The Dilemma
of the Modern
Jew

The Dilemma of the Modern Jew

by Joachim Prinz

LITTLE, BROWN AND COMPANY

BOSTON • TORONTO

The author wishes to thank the following for permission to use
copyrighted material:

Harper & Brothers for an excerpt from TRIAL AND ERROR by
Chaim Weizmann.

Random House, Inc. for "Israel" (POEMS 1940-1953) by Karl
Shapiro. Copyright 1948 by Karl Shapiro. Reprinted from POEMS
OF A JEW, by Karl Shapiro, by permission of Random House, Inc.
Originally appeared in *The New Yorker*. Also for an excerpt from
the Introduction to POEMS OF A JEW, Karl Shapiro. © Copyright
1958 by Karl Shapiro. Reprinted from the Introduction to POEMS
OF A JEW, by Karl Shapiro, by permission of Random House, Inc.

University of Chicago Press for an excerpt from THE GHETTO
by Louis Wirth, copyright 1928 by University of Chicago.

Yale University Press for an excerpt from PSYCHOANALYSIS
AND RELIGION by Eric Fromm, 1950.

Published simultaneously in Canada
by Little, Brown & Company (Canada) Limited

PRINTED IN THE UNITED STATES OF AMERICA

FOR HILDE

The Promise

of

Equality

THE BIRTHDAY OF THE MODERN JEW IS September 28, 1791. The birthplace is Paris, and the sociopolitical setting is the French Revolution. It was on that day that the Jews of France became citizens of the newly created Republic of France. This was the signal for the great historic development which goes under the name of the Emancipation of the Jews. Emancipation has created an opportunity for development for the Jews which makes of it one of the most important turning points in the entire Jewish history. Much criticism has been advanced in the last fifty years of the difficulties, the dilemmas and the hypocrisies which were the direct consequence of the Emancipation. But nobody can deny that every contemporary Jewish movement, political and religious, indeed almost every type of Jewish institution in the world today, owes its existence to the Emancipation. Actually the whole posture of the modern Jew, his outlook on life, his concept of himself, his conduct in both the affairs of his people and his own affairs, let alone his cultural and moral makeup, are based on the fact that he is, *de jure* and *de facto,* an emancipated Jew, a citizen of the country in which he lives.

The era of Emancipation constitutes as much of a

completely and radically new chapter as the era of Ezra. In many respects it is a second exodus from Egypt with consequences of tremendous importance. This is the real meaning of the twenty-eighth of September, 1791.

For those who are familiar with the social philosophy upon which the French Revolution was based, and without which it could not have taken place, the Emancipation must seem like a foregone conclusion. They must be surprised to learn that it came so late, not at the very beginning in 1789, but fully two years later, and after a prolonged and at times bitter debate in the Assemblée Nationale, the parliament of the New Republic. The lateness of the declaration is indeed of great symptomatic importance. It was due to the anti-Semitic agitation of some political leaders, and was the result of busy agitation of representatives from Alsace-Lorraine who translated the French word for Jew, *juif,* into "usurer." ("To jew" in English still means that.) Yet, late or not, the debate finally ended with the victory of the liberal forces bent upon full emancipation.

The motion which carried at long last was based on views expressed by the liberal Clermont-Tonnerre. It has by now become one of the famous sentences of Jewish history. It was to dominate the discussion of the "glory and misery" of the era of Emancipation which agitated the Jewish mind toward the end of

the nineteenth century. It was called a blessing as well
as a curse, and it was probably both. The motion,
accepted by a vast majority, read: *"To the Jews as
human beings — everything, to the Jews as a nation —
nothing.* They must become citizens. Some say that
the Jews will not accept citizenship. Let them declare
themselves clearly. If they cannot be citizens, they
must be expelled from this country. We cannot tolerate
a nation within a nation." * This sentence must be
read and reviewed in its contemporary context, lest
it be misunderstood. The term "Jews as a nation" was
a common expression of the century. When Immanuel
Kant, the great Prussian philosopher, defended his
thesis as a young professor of the University of Koe-
nigsberg, one of his two academic "opponents" was
listed as "Dr. Marcus Herz of the Jewish nation."
Nation in this contemporary concept of the eighteenth
century means a national and ethnic group. The
Emancipation, of course, did not happen suddenly.
The Revolution had not been fought merely for the
purpose of being charitable to the Jews. As a matter
of fact, the Emancipation was not at all a present to
the Jews, given to them in the spirit of tolerance
and benevolence; it was a necessity for the new state.

In 1791 the Jews of France, as indeed of much of
Europe, were very much part of the landscape. They

* From Clermont-Tonnerre's speech, delivered December 23,
1789.

had lived in France for almost seventeen hundred years, and in some countries (in Italy, for instance) since the days before Christ. The French Revolution simply had to deal with them, not in terms of charity or grace, but in terms of the modern state which it created, unless it decided to kill them off. The Jews were the only group within the state that had enjoyed a special status for centuries. There was no other group like them. Economically, they might have been considered middle-class, and therefore part of the *tiers état* which had carried the Revolution. Indeed, many Jews fought on the barricades of Paris before 1791. But they fought as patriots, not as citizens. The constitutional question was not so easily decided. The transfer from their status as a nation apart from the rest of the nation to full citizenship required a great deal more consideration.

Throughout the Middle Ages, that great era of Christian creativity, the Jews enjoyed a special legal and economic status. In a Christian society they could not possibly become an integral part of either the medieval state or the Christian society. Conversion to Christianity remedied this situation from one day to the other. But the Jews (with very few exceptions) chose not to convert. To the medieval state based upon the principles of the Christian Church, the Jews were infidels and were treated as such. Since the medieval state was based on law and order, a special status had to be created for the Jews. This special status was expressed in a number of severe restrictions: a special quarter of the town was designated as the ghetto, a number of economic pursuits both in agriculture and the crafts were not available to Jews. But in spite of all this, the special status of the Jews also meant protection. Contrary to all popular notions about that era, it remains a historic fact that the Jews were not merely a persecuted but also a privileged national group. It is true that very often they were dependent upon the whims and moods of dukes and counts, but they were nevertheless protected by the special status of a corporate society within the state. They had their own jurisdiction, their autonomous administration, their own language and, of course, their own civilization, religious and secular. The French Revolution, which formulated the foundations upon which the modern state was to rest, had no other choice but to declare null and void both the privileges accorded to a special group and the existence of the special corporate group itself. The French simply had to emancipate the Jews whether they liked it or not. Emancipation in the case of the Jews meant not merely the liberation of the Jews from medieval restrictions, but also from the special status bestowed upon them by the historic necessities of the medieval state. No such privileged group, no such "corporate society," could possibly be tolerated in the modern state.

There are, of course, ideological reasons which must be added. In an era which proclaimed reason as the only basis of human existence, emancipating the Jews seemed the only logical and reasonable thing to do. If Descartes was right in establishing the ability to think as the proof and the very meaning of human existence, Jews could not possibly be exempt from this universal rule. If it was to be universal, it had to be all-embracing. It was almost a matter of logical syllogism. Since all men were equal, Jews, being human, had to be accorded equality. To the revolutionary philosophers, the disciples of Descartes, Voltaire and Locke, it seemed that simple. It was, as we shall see, not that simple. But in the light of both the philosophy of reason and the concept of the modern state, the emancipation of the Jews was inevitable.

The reaction, at least at first, was tumultuous. The Middle Ages had finally been overcome, a new era of understanding had begun, the old hatreds and prejudices were forgotten, and there was to be but one humanity. Beethoven's Ninth Symphony, which ends with Schiller's "Ode to Joy," and the proclamation that "all people are now brethren," is probably the best expression of this mood. There was no doubt in the minds of either the revolutionaries or the beneficiaries of the Revolution that this was the year *one* in the history of mankind, and that from now on all those distinctions of religion, race or nationality which separate people would disappear because it was the most, in fact the only, reasonable thing to do. As the ornaments disappeared from the prerevolutionary rococo style of the furniture, as architecture straightened out and shed the "nonsensical" embellishments of the eighteenth-century baroque, so would all things become simpler, more straightforward, including human relations. When the great Cathedral of Reims was closed for a time and a big *To Let* sign was placed in front of its magnificent portal, a new period of history had finally and definitely come, an era when Reason should reign supreme. The Jews therefore had nothing to fear. Reason would do away with all that irrational nonsense which had excluded them so cruelly from the great benefit of being free and happy like all the others.

But Napoleon's attitude toward the Jews was ambivalent, to say the least. He decided to play two different roles in the settlement of the Jewish problem during the dramatic years after the Revolution. He wanted to be known as the liberator of the Jews, particularly in those countries which his armies overran and in which he was able to establish a French administration. (Russia was, of course, not one of them, although Napoleon's name is often used in the Jewish folklore of that time.) On the other hand, he was determined to be the stern administrator and executor of Clermont-Tonnerre's conditional emancipation: *"To the Jews as human beings — everything, to the Jews as a nation — nothing."* It is interesting that Napoleon should have interpreted this formula as a kind of conditional surrender, the condition being that the Jews would give up their own national life and, as a reward, receive equality of rights.

Since Napoleon had a sense of history and was sure to be writing the most glorious pages of French and European history himself, he was fond of theatrics for the sake of their dramatic effect. This affected his attitude toward the Jews as well. It is now almost forgotten that during his conquest of Egypt in 1799 he paused long enough to issue a solemn invitation to the Jewish people to return to their ancient homeland, Palestine, and rebuild it. He thus became the first Zionist of the nineteenth century, some seventy-five years before Theodor Herzl. In France itself his actions toward the Jews were dictated by two considerations: He was determined to bring the Emancipation to an orderly and lawful conclusion, once and for all. By contrast, he was impressed by reports from Alsace-Lorraine, where large parts of the population, particularly the rural population, were indebted to the Jews who for centuries had acted as moneylenders. As is always the case, creditors were seldom liked, particularly if the rate of interest was high and if they were Jews. The situation was a hangover from pre-Emancipation days, when moneylending was one of the few occupations open to Jews. It was profitable though, and Jews apparently hung on to it. The bad impression which these urgent reports made (and Alsace-Lorraine was a politically important province) was aggravated even more by information which reached Napoleon during his military campaigns, alleging that Jewish peddlers had been following his armies steadfastly, and that the soldiers complained about having been shortchanged by them and sold inferior merchandise to boot. These reports, coming from the officers of an army in combat, seemed to Napoleon a graphic illustration and indeed proof of the immoral conduct of the Jews in Alsace-Lorraine.

To determine the status of the Jews, both individually and collectively, within the new postrevolutionary French state, Napoleon called two meetings. The first — held in 1806 and heralded as the "Assemblée des Notables" — called the leaders of the Jewish communities of France together for a discussion of the future relationship of the Jewish communities with the French government and the organization of the Jewish community itself. But this meeting was a mere rehearsal. The spectacular show was to be held a year later. With typical sense of drama and history, it was called "Sanhedrin," in memory of the Supreme Court of Jewish antiquity. As the ancient court had met in pomp and circumstance, seventy-one in number, so was the imperial invitation sent to seventy-one Jewish leaders. All seventy-one appeared dutifully and mindful of the role which they were to play. As if they had to be reminded of the solemnity that was to follow, they were provided with velvet caps and gowns. Indeed, so much was made of the occasion that everybody expected the Emperor himself to preside over the meetings. Napoleon, who had made all these theatrical suggestions, had long forgotten both the date and the purpose of the meeting. An official by the name of Molé, himself a half-Jew and a convert, conducted the meeting. The meeting was more like a performance, and had both its tragic and its comic aspects.

Molé, comically oblivious of his own Jewish family background, acted like a stern father admonishing his children not to deviate from the straight and narrow path prescribed by the Act of Emancipation. The aim was obvious from the very beginning: from now on Jewish activities were to be restricted to religious life. Even in their religious functions and, above all, in their religious principles, the real aim was final disintegration. Everything that served this goal was to be encouraged. Everything that seemed to deter it was to be eliminated. Never before had the philosophy of assimilation as a goal devoutly to be desired been more clearly defined. Since the assembly consisted of both secular and rabbinic leaders (we have several portraits of some of the gentlemen, and they look very dignified and impressive), it was not easy for Molé to exact clear answers to the rather blunt questions: Would the Jews object to mixed marriages? Would the rabbis, in fact, solemnize such marriages? Would they be encouraged or looked upon with disdain? Did the Jews look upon themselves as a chosen people? There were twelve such questions. The answers were not always easy to give. Everyone was aware of what was being played here and that the stakes were high. On the other hand, the answers, although cleverly formulated if not forthright, had to be at least truthful. There was enough supervision to make certain that promises would be kept. When the guarded answers to the first eleven queries were given, the last one was posed dramatically: Do you or your people consider any country outside of France your fatherland? The seventy-one robed gentlemen rose to their feet and solemnly assured the Emperor's deputy that there was but one fatherland, France, and they broke into an awe-inspiring *Vive la France* and sang the militant song of the Revolution, "La Marseillaise," which had become France's national anthem. Not a pretty scene. Lack of sincerity and understanding of the complexity of the problems had dominated both the questions and the answers. History was to prove both wrong. The only concrete, and not unimportant, result of the "Sanhedrin" was the creation of the "Consistoire des Israélites de France." The word *juifs*

(Jews) was not used in good society at the time, either in France or in other countries. The central religious body of the Jews of France had thus come into being, a model for many other countries. The body exists and functions to this very day.

With the Jews of Alsace-Lorraine, Napoleon was much less ceremonial. The debts incurred by the Alsatian peasants were simply canceled. An imperial decree, known in Jewish history as the "Décret Infâme," directed the debtors not to pay a single penny which they owed to Jewish moneylenders. In no court of law would such an arbitrary act be upheld. But there was no such court. If the Emancipation was to be understood in terms of equality before the law, it was indeed a very bad beginning.

This act was in itself a blow to both the letter and the spirit of the Emancipation. It was, however, not merely the whimsical act of a dictatorial Emperor. It was in keeping with the tendencies of the time. The Emancipation was proclaimed practically everywhere in Western Europe. But the governments which had issued these proclamations felt that the complete implementation of the new laws was out of step with public opinion. In one of the most interesting debates held in Berlin on the further implementation of the Prussian Act of Emancipation of 1812, this point is made again and again. The participants were members of the Upper Chamber, noblemen, well educated and well meaning. Many of them express very liberal thoughts both on the status of the Jews and in their interpretation of the functions of the state. Nobody, in fact, doubts the *justice* of the Emancipation. But when it comes to granting an extension of the already granted civil rights, they balk. There is, they say, some difference between justice and *wisdom*. However *just* it was to admit the Jews to citizenship, it would not be *wise* to extend their rights and privileges now. The emphasis was on *now*. Later, perhaps. Progress should be gradual so as to give the people time to "catch up with the new times."

We live in a Christian state [said Count Solms-Baruth in this debate] and I believe it to be our duty to approach the problem in due acknowledgment of this fact. In spite of our desire to exercise the most liberal tolerance, we must be sure that this is done step by step. Until now the Jews have lived in rather restricted circumstances concerning their civil and political rights. The department [of the government] submits a law which would extend their civil rights; it has appealed to us to adopt its recommendation and has made reference to moral status of the Jews. The department itself admonishes us to be cautious and counsels that their [the Jews'] admission to greater civil rights be gradual. But to make them the equals of their Christian fellow citizens, the majority opinion of the members of the department does not think commensurate with the state of civilization among the bulk of the Jewish population. It is for these reasons that I would warn this Assembly to go carefully and cautiously about this matter, and to grant to the Jews only those rights which were submitted and suggested by the rapporteur. It is indeed a transition from their former situation and a step toward further equalization with their Christian fellow citizens. If the government feels that the Jews are only capable to assume responsibilities in a certain number of specific civil services and not in others, it expresses an opinion. This opinion is that this legislation should be considered the beginning of a longer process and that it would be inadvisable to tear down completely the barriers which separate Jews from Christians. Yet, a beginning it is and a good beginning and one which augurs well for further measures of emancipation at a later time.

I have quoted these interesting observations *in toto* not merely because the document is hardly known, but because it is characteristic of the arguments of the period. We must not forget that the Holy Alliance, formed at the Congress of Vienna, marks the reestablishment of the Christian state. The head of the state was also the official leader of the church. The concept of the Christian state itself was a far cry from the purely secular and even antireligious, and certainly anticlerical, ideas of the French Revolution. In the debate from which I quoted, the *rapporteur* of the legislation made some interesting references to the separation of church and state in the United States and added significantly: "For the time being, however, our state is not so constituted as in the United States of America where state and church are in fact separated. And I am deeply convinced that *even if this were a desirable goal,* it would take quite some time before we would be able to attain it. As long as this is not the case, the opinions of fifteen million Christians must be taken into serious consideration."

The trend is now clear. The *vox populi* has to be regarded as a very important, perhaps the determining, factor. What is advised is gradual liberalization with due respect to popular opinion. The popular opinion, to say it quite bluntly, is against the Jews. It is anti-Semitic.

The decades which follow, between 1815 and the turn of the century, are not easily described. It would be unfair to see them as a succession of anti-Semitic movements and even riots. It would be equally inaccurate to view them merely in terms of actual progress of the Jewish emancipation. In fact, both progress and regression took place, but they often occurred simultaneously. The writing of the history of the post-Emancipation era has sometimes been done in tendentious terms. This is a legitimate use of history for purposes of *propaganda.* For the sake of *historic truth,* however, we must understand that this is a highly complex, many-colored, many-sided story of a dynamic and often fluid development.

Since there will be many dark pages in this story, it is well to begin with the credit side of the account. It must be said that the progress toward full emancipation which was achieved in a very short time simply seems incredible. The rise of emancipated Jewry in the world is probably one of the most outstanding phenomena in history. The young generation, born in freedom, took to the new life with vigor and enthusiasm.

There were, of course, elders among the Jews who cautioned against the enthusiasm of the young. They foresaw all kinds of disadvantages which would accrue from this newfangled thing called Emancipation: military service, the sacrifice of the privilege of self-administration; and last, but not least, the question of Jewish survival under the new regime was raised. But these old-timers were soon silenced; they were told they did not understand that a new, a brand-new, time had come and that indeed something like the Messianic era had arrived. There was something of that in the Jewish attitude, as there always is. The Jews are strangely and profoundly addicted to Messianism. But who can blame them? Here they had hardly emerged from the ghetto, and were already taking hold of their new life, not merely in France, but in other countries as well. Although the decrees of emancipation did not come immediately everywhere, they were soon issued and became the law of the land.

Soon, very soon, with almost unbelievable yet characteristic speed and enthusiasm, the Jews embraced this new life and entered their new, unaccustomed career as citizens of these countries.

We must admire the spirit in which the Jewish generation in all the countries that had finally been granted emancipation assumed the duties of their new citizenship and seized every opportunity to avail themselves of the new challenges. Of course, there were always, even before the Emancipation, a few privileged groups. It had always been different in Spain under the Moslem rulers, with whose help the Jews had created a golden era of literature and art, not merely for themselves but for the whole country. The persecutions and final expulsion occurred only after the Christian reconquest. In Holland, where Jews had found refuge from the Inquisition of Spain and Portugal, they lived in great comfort; after all, Spinoza lived in the seventeenth century, and not in the nineteenth century, and had the Jews themselves not excommunicated him, he would have been buried with honors in a Jewish cemetery. There were privileged, preemancipated Jews in Prussia and Austria. The decree of 1750, under the reign of Frederick the Great, had granted privileges to some Jews of Berlin so that the *salons* of the literary world were presided over by Jewish ladies dressed in crinolines and by their husbands, looking like the gentlemen of the eighteenth century. There was Moses Mendelssohn, the philosopher, an intimate friend of the great Kant, and the even more popular Gotthold Ephraim Lessing. Salamone Rossi was a respected composer and the head of the chamber music group at the ducal palace in Mantua, Italy; in Austria, Jews who helped finance the Thirty Years' War were even knighted by imperial decree.

But all these were exceptions. Certain Jews had privileges; none had rights. But now the rights had been extended to all. One of the first things to be done was the adjustment of religious life to the new conditions. Orthodox Judaism, the Judaism of the "revealed law," found itself suddenly deprived of its very foundations. The legal autonomy was gone. There were no longer Jewish courts of any validity outside of rabbinical courts of mere arbitration in religious matters. The authority of the Jewish law in civil and criminal matters had been replaced by the public courts of the state. Jewish weddings could no longer be performed "in accordance with the law of Moses and Israel" unless they were first certified by the state. A Jewish wedding therefore was no longer a *legal* act but a Jewish *solemnization* of a civil act performed by the authorities of the state. This was true also of Jewish divorces, of the law governing inheritance, and certainly of criminal law. The Jewish prisons, like that in the former ghetto of Prague, became museum pieces.

Orthodoxy became merely *orthopraxy*. The transition
from ghetto orthodoxy to the neo-orthodoxy of
the nineteenth century was theologically guided by
Frankfurt's eminent Rabbi Samson Rafael Hirsch.

Altogether, the inner adjustment came from Germany, not from France or from any other country.
Those who have undertaken to analyze the strange
phenomenon that was German Jewry have been
either romanticists or people who suffered from the
malady of resentment. Neither approach will do justice to the historic role which German Jewry played
in both the nineteenth and twentieth centuries. Actually, all contemporary movements were originally conceived by German Jewry. We are concerned here not
with the reasons but with the facts. Thus we must
state that as neo-orthodoxy stemmed from Frankfurt,
so did liberal Judaism (called Reform in America)
come from Hamburg. The first synagogue in which
an organ was played (Orthodox Jews, like Christian
fundamentalists in America's Bible Belt, disdain organ music on the Sabbath) was in Seesen, Germany;
the most important liberal temple was in Hamburg. Nor was the use of the organ and the mixed
choir (Orthodox Jews are opposed to men singing
with women, even for the glory of God) the most important precept of the new liberal school. A new "theology" was created. The tradition was viewed in terms
of its viability in these new days of freedom. Much of

the old tradition had to be rejected. Hebrew liturgy was adjusted not merely to Jewish needs but to Protestant usage. Political considerations sometimes guided the hands and words of theologians, and Isaiah began to sound like the rationalistic prophets of the French Revolution. But all this does not mean that reform was not necessary, or that nobody gave serious consideration to its real meaning within the framework of the new conditions. Abraham Geiger of Wiesbaden, a very great scholar, became the leader of the movement which, under the leadership of Isaac M. Wise and Samuel Holdheim, became such an important force in the United States.

During the passionate battle between the Orthodox Jews and the Reformers (much can be read about it in Heine's prose and verse), Zacharias Frankel of Breslau offered a new solution, that of the "historic school," which rejected both Orthodoxy and Reform and held a position very much between them. It has become the Conservative movement as we understand it in America, although even its adherents have found it increasingly difficult to find a clear definition. Yet sometimes movements prove to be viable in spite of a lack of definition simply because they perform a function. Frankel's historic Judaism is one of them.

These religious changes could not have taken place without the foundation born of the necessities of the day and of the inevitable historic constellation which is known under the untranslatable German term of *Wissenschaft des Judentums*. Far from being a "science," it was the sheer necessity of creating the scholastic instruments that would enable the new post-Emancipation generation to understand Judaism as religion and as history in intelligible, modern terms. There existed, of course, no Jewish history, no Jewish philology other than the endeavors of the medieval grammarians, no bibliography of the vast mass of Jewish literature. Under the guidance of Leopold Zunz, Moritz Steinschneider and others, the *Wissenschaft* furnished the foundation without which neither Graetz nor Dubnow could have written their voluminous histories of the Jewish people.

Socially and economically, the progress was incredible. The synagogue, once an inconspicuous building relegated to the hidden and unknown precincts of the ghetto, now became part of the architectural landscape of every city. The nineteenth century, for some strange reason, preferred a mixed and ill-defined Moorish style, which can still be seen in Paris, in Budapest and in some of the old German Jewish synagogues in the United States. (In Germany the synagogues were all destroyed in 1938.) The Star of David, the *Magen David*, never before an important Jewish symbol, now dominated the domes of the synagogues, as the cross dominated the churches. The Jews themselves had become the neighbors of their Christian fellow citizens. There were rarely enough Jews to form a Jewish neighborhood in the American sense. (Vienna was probably the exception.) Jewish merchants, physicians and lawyers became increasingly popular with the people — the lawyer surrounded with the halo of particular shrewdness, the Jewish doctor benefiting from the old tradition of Jewish physicians of the Middle Ages. In reality, their very popularity — or rather the irrational reasons for their popularity — was in itself attributable to deep-seated anti-Semitic notions. This phenomenon alone would be a worthwhile study in perverted anti-Semitism.

Young Jewish people attended public school with their Christian classmates more often than not, particularly in small towns, where there were very few of them. There were as yet no Jewish professors, at least not in German universities, unless they had converted to Christianity. But there was a large number of Jewish academic teachers in all the countries of Emancipation, and in some rare instances, even in Russia. The Jews were conscripted into the armies, and in some countries they even became officers. In literature and the arts they began to make their contributions, although their larger participation begins in the twentieth century. Since we deal here only (at least for the time being) with the nineteenth century, the names of Heinrich Heine in literature, of

Mendelssohn, Meyerbeer and Offenbach in music, and of Camille Pissarro in painting must suffice. Of course, Felix Mendelssohn-Bartholdy, Moses Mendelssohn's grandson, had been baptized at birth. But when the great Goethe heard him play the violin, he exclaimed, "What a talented Jew boy." Water, however sacred, remains water after all. Another generation had to be born in order to produce a Modigliani and a Chagall, a Franz Kafka and an André Maurois, a Gustav Mahler and a Schoenberg.

Much of the ghetto mentality was also gone. The Jewish communities, not only in France, were publicly recognized corporate societies and enjoyed the protection of the law. In some countries, the rabbis were paid by the state and were treated as civil servants. The communities levied taxes upon their members which became full-fledged obligations collected by the state authorities together with the public taxes. There no longer was any sense of fear when complaints had to be lodged in the courts. Yet the old medieval institution of *shtadlanut* remained; the representatives of the communities were men of social and financial influence. Infringements upon the rights of the Jews were openly and frankly criticized, and the courageous example of Gabriel Riesser, who fought in the Prussian Parliament for Jewish rights, was emulated by many Jewish political party leaders. It is interesting to note that it was Gabriel Riesser who used the word "Jew" again instead of the cowardly "Israelite." He named a journal published by him in 1860 *Der Jude*. When Martin Buber published his famous monthly in 1916 under this name, it had a completely different connotation.

The average Jew in Germany, France, England, Holland and all the other Western countries (Austria and Hungary have to be treated separately, since the pattern of Jewish life changed considerably as soon as one left Vienna and Budapest, the capitals) was contented, patriotic and middle-class. There was hardly a Jewish proletariat. Of course, there was anti-Semitism. Fraternities did not accept Jews. At some universities there existed a *numerus clausus*. Jewish soldiers were rarely promoted unless there was a war. Social life was largely restricted to Jewish friends and neighbors, although there were cases of Christian-Jewish friendship. Anti-Semitic incidents occurred in schools, instigated not only by the students but often by the teachers. For a Jew to pass by a table in the *Bierkellers* when a heated political debate was held was not particularly pleasant, and even during public debates in Parliament anti-Semitic speeches could be heard. But in spite of all this (some of my readers may have compared some of these descriptions with present-day America and will have found familiar traits), life was quite peaceful. In later years, particularly during the bloody Hitler regime, Jews were heard saying that they were longing "for the good old days of anti-Semitism." Anti-Semitism without gas chambers seemed paradise.

But while the good, patriotic Jewish burgher was happily contemplating the future of his children and grandchildren in those days when anti-Semitism would have surely disappeared, the objective observer of the Jewish scene of the nineteenth century felt less serene. In France, Germany, Holland, Austria-Hungary and England, those countries which had either proclaimed emancipation and promulgated specific laws concerning the status of the Jews, there lived only slightly over a million Jews. The majority of the Jewish people, some six million, lived in Eastern Europe, which includes Romania. In these countries only a relatively small group of successful merchants and professional men were privileged to live in the large cities, unmolested and enjoying a degree of equality. But it was a privilege, not a right. In none of these countries had emancipatory laws been issued. Russia and Poland had the largest concentration of Jews in the world at that time (American Jewry was small and insignificant in those days); they were forced to live in small towns with hardly any Christian population at all. Those *shtetls* (townlets) had their romantic aspects and became the subject of Sholem Aleichem's delightful, humorous stories and Chagall's marvelously colorful canvases. They produced an amazingly rich creativity in folk music and religious learning. But they were in fact the result of a deliberate act of humiliation, and the misery and deprivation which the Jewish people endured in these little towns were indescribable. The Russian ghetto, or "Pale of Settlement," was the result of deliberate anti-Semitic policy on the part of the Russian government. This is in fact the characteristic of Eastern European anti-Semitism: It was not merely a popular reaction. It was an integral part of the official policy of the government. The heads of the governments, the members of the parliaments, the official bureaucracy, the civil service and the clergy — they all were uncompromisingly anti-Semitic. It is for this reason that all the problems and solutions which were indicated for the West had no validity for the East, and that I have to deal with these countries separately and specifically. For the Jews in Eastern Europe the Middle Ages had not yet ended.

The Russian situation presents a picture of confusion and inconsistencies. It is difficult to understand that Russia was part of the same continent which had produced the French Revolution and the spirit of the nineteenth century. This is, of course, true of its government, its literature and its philosophy. The evolutionary process which made possible the transition from the autocratic class society of the Middle Ages to the democratic society of our time was imperceptible in Russia. Little, if any, of the light of the movement of reason penetrated the towns and villages of mother Russia. The group of enlightened and educated people remained small. Political alertness and participation in government were restricted to a few, and every move toward broadening the base and involving the people was considered high treason. The Czar and his throne were surrounded by the most brutal of bodyguards for fear that the discontented might come too close. The masses of the people had enshrined him in godlike fashion in the icons of their hearts and elevated him to the position of the all-knowing father married to mother Russia, infallible and entitled to every possible whim.

In such an atmosphere the Jews could not possibly fare well. Even after the serfs had been emancipated and a new class, the burghers, began to emerge, there was no emancipation of the Jews at all. Some of the Czars felt rather generous when they permitted some wealthy Jews to move to large cities and enjoy the Russian version of equality. There were indeed Jews with large holdings and considerable economic influence: the Efrosis of Odessa, Baron Horace de Guinsburg, the Poliakovs, all of them private bankers in the Rothschild tradition. Some were active and even leading in the building of railroads. But the numbers were pitifully small. When the first decree (in 1819) permitted merchants of the "first guild" to leave the Pale of Settlement and move permanently to the large cities, only one hundred and ninety Jews met the requirements. This small number must be compared with a Jewish population of 5,215,805 in 1897. The misery and degradation of the Jewish masses defy imagination and description. It is simply impossible to conceive of such conditions: human beings subjected to every possible humiliation, personal and collective, yet living, after all, on the European continent, just a few hundred miles from Paris and Berlin. The government considered the Jews morally incurable, and this premise, rarely doubted, led to a policy which relegated the masses to an area of 362,000 square miles, where they lived under such economic and social conditions that the medieval ghettos seemed paradise indeed. When in 1898 Konstantin Petrovich Pobyedonostzev, the tutor of Czar Alexander III and the head of the Holy Synod, received a Jewish delegation, his prognosis for Russian Jewry was: "One third will die, one third will leave the country, and the rest will be completely absorbed." Much later, in the 1920's, similar thoughts were expressed by the anti-Semitic Prime Minister of Poland, Colonel Beck, who did not hesitate to state publicly that two thirds of Poland's three and a half million Jews were "superfluous."

From the very beginning of the nineteenth century, Russia approached the problem of Jewish emancipation in its own strange manner. Jews, the Russian government claimed, were of such low moral character that emancipation was practically impossible. Those who were found morally capable of citizenship had to forswear any kind of allegiance to ancient Jewish custom. The Jews themselves showed little inclination to disagree with the government. While Jews in Western countries fought for equality of rights to be accorded to all Jews, Russian Jewry accepted the theory that the masses could not be emancipated and pleaded for toleration and rights for the privileged class of Jews. In a petition addressed to Czar Alexander II (in June, 1856) we read: "Were the new generation which has been brought up in the spirit and under the control of the government, were the higher mercantile class which has for many years diffused life, activity and wealth in the land . . . to receive from the government as a mark of distinction, greater rights than those who have done nothing to attest their loyalty, usefulness and industry, then the whole Jewry . . . would joyfully hasten to attain the goal marked by the government." What was demanded by the Jews themselves was not emancipation of all the Jews, but "equal rights with the other subjects to the well educated and well deserving Jews who possess the title of honorary citizens, to the merchants affiliated for a number of years with the first and second guild and distinguished by their business integrity, as well as to

the soldiers who have served honorably in the army."
The Jewish petition proceeds to ask that equality be
accorded "to the best of us." No Jewish community
in the West had ever degraded itself to that extent.
No Western government, of course, could be compared with the czarist regime in Russia and the combined rule of army and church. The "Committee for
the Amelioration of the Jews" which had been appointed in 1802, and had been reappointed from
time to time, addressed itself to this problem alone.
The matter of the Pale of Settlement and the fate of
the millions of starving Jews there was not their concern. After three years of discussion the petition was
granted, and in 1859 the Czar sanctioned the decision,
which became the law of the land, that "Jewish merchants who have belonged to the first guild for not less
than two years . . . shall be permitted to settle permanently in the interior of the country," namely, outside of the ghetto area. However, if they should fail
to meet the payments stipulated for these merchants,
"they shall be sent back to the Pale." What was thus
granted was not equality for all, but toleration for
the selected few.

It would be unfair to overlook the fact that there
were a few lonely voices in Russia, even among the
aristocrats, who understood that this was the nineteenth and not the thirteenth century. Count Stroganof, the Minister of the Interior, during a period

when there was some hope for a more adequate and equitable solution of the Jewish problem, had suggested that "restrictions which go only half way or are externally imposed by the police are not sufficient to direct this huge mass of people towards useful occupations." He even went so far as to plead the cause of the Jews in terms of Christian inhumanity: "With the patience of martyrs the Jews of Western Europe had endured the most atrocious persecutions, and had yet succeeded in keeping their natural type intact until the governments took the trouble to inquire more deeply into the causes separating the Jews from general civic life, so as to be able to attack the causes themselves." His general recommendations, however, pointed in the usual direction: removal of Jewish tradition, segregation of the incurable masses and abolition of Jewish self-government in their religious and cultural concerns. In the following decades, the human preamble of these recommendations was soon forgotten and all that was left was hatred, brutality and organized murder.

The beginnings of the reign of Alexander II (1855) were marked by a new, hopeful liberalism. Censorship was relaxed, and newspapers enjoyed a spell of comparative freedom. A redistribution of land promised a new and better life for the peasants, who were emancipated by special decree. Reforms in the judiciary system and in local governments seemed sure signs of the beginning of a new, liberal era. There was hope even for the Jews. Count Stroganof, the Governor of New Russia, went so far as to declare: "The existence in our times of restrictions in the rights of the Jews as compared with the Christian population in any shape or form is neither in accord with the spirit and tendency of the age, nor with the policy of the government looking forward towards the amalgamation of the Jews with the native population of the Empire." His remained a lone voice. Nevertheless, new Jewish groups (artisans, pharmacists, midwives) were added to those permitted to leave the Pale and settle elsewhere in the country. Some of the most humiliating restrictions were lifted. The city of Vilna, for instance, was no longer permitted to exclude Jews from certain streets. As a result of the newly established local governments, Jews began to participate in rural assemblies and were even elected to offices. Some primary schools were opened to Jewish children. Altogether, the Russian school system was now considered the best medium for the assimilation of the Jews.

This liberal spirit, which filled so many Jews with hope for final emancipation, ended more abruptly than it had begun. While the Jews would have been satisfied with the slightest relaxation of the restrictive laws, the people of Russia, particularly the intelligentsia, were clamoring for constitutional government and complete liberal reforms. These were the days when the Narodniki, the thousands of Russian students, would roam the countryside to "discover the people." These were the days of social and anarchist groups dreaming of liberation from the yoke of the czars. Leo Tolstoy had already published his *War and Peace* and *Anna Karenina*. It was during the reign of Alexander II that his "conversion" to the social gospel of Christianity took place. His *Confessions* were written in 1879. Dostoevsky's great novels revealed the mystical depth and the social meaning of the Russian national character. Prince Peter Krapotkin joined the anarchistic student movement. As these new radical forces began to make themselves felt, the Pan-Slavic movement began to exert its influence upon the government. More and more must the police be entrusted with the "solution" of the burning social issues of the time. This "solution" meant imprisonment in countless jails, deportation to Siberia and merciless killings. Of the Narodniki alone (altogether a group of two or three thousand people), seven hundred and seventy were arrested, and two hundred and fifteen sent to prisons. Hundreds were punished in other ways. (The socialist hopes were shared by some Jews. Ansky, the author of *The Dybbuk,* was one of the Narodniki.) Police protection was the more urgent because the life of the Czar was in danger. Two attempts to assassinate him had failed. On

March 13, 1881, the anarchists succeeded. Alexander was killed. With his death begins the most tragic chapter in the history of Russian Jewry.

To Alexander III, a man of considerable physical strength (he bragged that he was able to bend a horseshoe with his bare hands), his father's violent death had proved that his liberal policies were wrong. Whatever his personal attachment to his father was, his reign began with the "Manifesto of Accession," which emphasized his "faith in the power and right of autocracy." A reign of terror began. The anarchists were to be demolished. The trains to Siberia were filled with them. Nevertheless, an early attempt upon the life of the young Czar was made which took the lives of twenty-one people but spared his. For a short while, some new liberal tendencies appeared in the government's dealings with the peasants. They soon gave way to complete reaction. The influence of Count Dmitri Tolstoy, who considered liberal concessions acts of weakness, soon became apparent. He was joined by the Czar's former teacher, Konstantin Pobyedonostzev, who was made Procurator of the Holy Synod and whose basic political philosophy was expressed in his *Moscow Conversations*. According to him, democracy was a rotten system leading to corruption. The press must be censored; it did not represent public opinion, anyway. Elections must be prevented. There must not be free speech. Even sermons must be submitted for censorship. Leo Tolstoy's adherents were to be prosecuted. The writer himself was excommunicated. Students' clubs were prohibited. If there were any disturbances at the universities, Cossacks were to be sent there with the clear instruction to use whips. With this kind of philosophy, which the young Czar eagerly accepted (his education was limited, his inclinations evil), what could the Jews expect?

It was an evil omen that among the group which had prepared the assassination was a Jewess named Hessia Helfmann. Although she had merely provided a hiding place for the revolutionaries, the Jews were to pay dearly for her "participation" in the plot. Count Nikolai Pavlovich Ignatiev was entrusted with the chairmanship of another "Central Committee for the Revision of the Jewish Question." Russia had more such committees than any other country. In the spring of 1882 the Ignatiev report was published. It became known and infamous in Jewish history as the preparation for the "May Laws" which changed the course of Jewish history. The "May Laws" restricted life in the Pale even further. It is unbelievable that a life already so completely fenced in could be reduced even further. But, apparently, even this was possible. This edict proclaimed that Jews who lived in the Pale were no longer permitted to reside in rural settlements. As a result of it, Jews had to move from the villages to the cities. The cities were already crowded. There was no opportunity to earn a living. The new arrivals did not merely aggravate the situation; they made it impossible. Odessa, which in 1847 had a Jewish population of 17,000, now (in 1897) had 138,715. Kiev, another Jewish center with a Jewish community of 3,013, grew to 31,801; and Moscow, from a tiny group of 300 to a community of 11,013.

Whenever a peasant decided that a Jew in his village was "vicious," he could expel him from his village without any further notice. Jews who — for reasons of business or family — left the village for but a few days were refused reentry. If a Jewish villager invited his widowed mother to move from her native village into his home, he was threatened with expulsion. If he were to leave his village for treatment in a hospital outside the village, he was not permitted to return. These laws were only applicable to villages. In order to expand their validity, many small towns were now declared to be villages so as to make it possible to apply the same anti-Semitic laws to them. No wonder Jews moved to cities. A general attack was now made on Jewish professionals. Many Jewish physicians lost their positions. The proportion of Jewish lawyers was lowered to 29 per cent. Those in excess of this quota were added to the growing number of unemployed and unemployable Jews. Artisans were subjected to restrictions, but they received permits for their work. As soon as an artisan acquired a machine for his shop, he was no longer considered an artisan but a manufacturer. There were no permits for manufacturers. It has been estimated that more than 40 per cent of Russian Jewry was dependent upon charity doled out by the few but very rich privileged Jews of the Jewish merchant-aristocracy. Their generosity was unparalleled in the history of private welfare.

The Ignatiev report was the strange reaction of the Russian government to the anti-Semitic outbreaks of 1881 which are known as pogroms, a Russian word meaning simply "disturbances." To the Jews and the civilized world they meant unbridled terror, instigated by the government and the church, with police and army standing idly by. Although such riots had taken place before in Russia (in 1821, 1859 and 1871), they were mere "incidents" as compared with the "era of pogroms" which began shortly after the assassination of Alexander II. It is of no small importance that the first of these bloody pogroms coincided with the Greek Orthodox Easter. It was an old medieval pattern. The Christian Church was very active in the reestablishment of the old czaristic autocracy. The famous "Manifesto of Accession," issued by Alexander III, which proclaimed the return to a policy of oppression and dictatorship, started with the pious words: "The voice of God hath commanded us to take up vigorously the rein of government." A systematic and vigorous action against Jews was begun by both the church and the "Sacred League," a terroristic, reactionary secret organization of which both Ignatiev and Pobyedonostzev were members. The church was busy spreading the anti-Semitic pamphlet *Concerning the use of Christian blood by the Jews* among the peasants. Those who could not read found policemen and agitators ready to read it to them. The newspapers, particularly in the south of Russia, began a systematic campaign of hatred and incitement to riots against the Jews. Rumors were spread that the life of the Czar had to be protected because the Jews were in possession of a "terrible secret." Agitators, sent by the reactionary group, appeared suddenly in places with a large Jewish population. The "spontaneous" outbreak of riots against Jews was carefully prepared. (Under the Hitler regime such outbursts of popular "spontaneity" led to the burning of synagogues during one night all over the country. The Russian pogroms had set a good example.) And the Greek Orthodox Easter of 1881 was the proper setting. The "enemies of Christianity and the Russian people" had to be destroyed. The first pogrom took place in Elizavetgrad on the fifteenth of April, 1881, a day to be remembered for a long time. The events had been carefully prepared. A drunkard was sent to one of the many Jewish saloons, there to sit and molest people. When the Jewish saloonkeeper removed the troublemaker from his place, he began to shout as he had been instructed: "The Jews are beating our people." It was the well-prepared signal for the pogrom. The soldiers and policemen had disappeared from the streets. The rabble took over. The pogrom had begun.

After Elizavetgrad (with a Jewish population of 15,000) came others: Kiev, first in the city itself, then in some fifty villages around the city; after that, towns and villages in Volhynia and Podolia; and finally in Odessa. The Jews were not altogether helpless. Jewish self-defense organizations sprang up wherever pogroms were expected. In the famous town of Berdichev, the mob which had arrived in freight cars was met at the station by Jewish youth armed with clubs, and was driven off. In Odessa, where the authorities behaved better than elsewhere, the young Jewish students were ready to meet the attackers, and prevented a disaster. Their grandchildren in spirit were later to lead the rebellion against the Nazi army in the Ghetto of Warsaw. Compared with Hitler's wholesale murders, the number of Jews who were killed and wounded during these pogroms seems insignificant. The damage inflicted upon property looms slightly greater. But the pogroms of 1881 and 1882 must be viewed as the culmination of a completely hopeless situation. The pogroms were but the bloody symbols of the utter lawlessness under which Russian Jews lived. The prisoners of the Pale of Settlement, who so far had been permitted to vegetate, were now deprived of the last vestige of rights, the right to live. There was little human dignity left. The pogroms sealed the doom of Russian Jewry. Only emigration could solve the problem. American Jewry was born in the blood-drenched streets of the pogromized towns of Russia.

The fateful year of 1881 was in its last month when another pogrom erupted, this time in Warsaw, the capital of the Polish kingdom. This came as a shock and surprise to the Jewish community because the Jews seemed to fare better in Poland than in Russia. Apparently, the pogrom was Russian-inspired, but the Poles themselves, from both the town and the surrounding villages, participated in it. It began, strangely enough, at Christmas services in the Cathedral of Warsaw. The church was filled with thousands of worshipers, when suddenly somebody cried out: "The church is on fire!" In the turmoil which followed, with the multitude pushing toward the church gates, several worshipers were trampled to death. In reality there was no fire, the rumor having been spread by pickpockets, who loved to take advantage of a confusion. When people became aware of this, a second rumor spread: "Two of the pickpockets were Jews." This, too, was later proved wrong, but it was too late. Whistles blew from somewhere. Hordes of strangers appeared, armed with clubs, and in no time at all they entered the Jewish quarters. For two long days there was destruction and terror among the Jews of Warsaw. When it all ended — with the police appearing, as usual, on the third day — fifteen hundred Jewish homes, stores and houses of worship had been demolished.

The Jews of Russia were stunned. Every semblance of security was now gone. If the Jews of Warsaw were not safe, then nobody was, anywhere. Public protest meetings were impossible. So the Jews, as in the Middle Ages, resorted to an ancient expression of anger, fear and despair. The eighteenth of January in 1882 was proclaimed a day of fasting and mourning, and heartbreaking scenes took place in the synagogues all over Russia, where all Jews assembled, rich and poor, privileged and oppressed. It was a solemn declaration of collective despair. Strangly enough, it made an impression upon the outside world. There were inquiries in England's House of Commons, with Gladstone's government reacting very cautiously. But there was a mass meeting in London's Mansion House, where leading clergymen (the Bishop of London and, most eloquently, the Roman Catholic Cardinal Manning) spoke out in terms of Christian outrage against the treatment of Jews. The tone was even more urgent and the government's attitude less timid in the United States, where the pogroms were denounced in both houses of Congress; a resolution passed by the House on February 23, 1883, called upon the Government of the United States to "exercise its influence with the Government of Russia to stay the spirit of persecution." Many speakers, both in Congress and at public meetings in New York, offered America as a haven of refuge.

Russia was not entirely impervious to public opinion in the world. The last pogrom took place in Balta (Podolia), with the terror again raging for the customary two days, with more than twelve hundred houses destroyed, but this time with a long list of Jews murdered, raped and driven to insanity. After this, a ukase by order of the Czar ended this first chapter of Russian terror. It was not until the infamous pogrom of Kishinev in 1903 that a new, even bloodier series of pogroms began. The end of pogroms brought no real change in the anti-Semitic policy of the Russian government or in the desperate mood of Russian Jewry. In 1891 during the days of Passover, a governmental edict expelled thousands of Jews from the city of Moscow. No reasons were given. Families who had lived there for decades were imprisoned and then released to be resettled in that huge crowded Pale of Settlement to starve, to despair and to die.

During the anti-Jewish propaganda in Russia, there were frequent references in the press and in official documents to "certain anti-Semitic movements abroad." That there were such movements outside of Russia was to make the Russian pogroms more respectable. These references, which never mentioned the country, pointed to the anti-Semitic movement in Germany, the ideological forerunner of the Nazis.

There were to be no pogroms in Germany, at least not for another half century. There was to be something much more enduring: anti-Semitism as a movement, based upon a philosophy, a *Weltanschauung* for the masses. The Germans, this unhappy "people of thinkers and poets," as they like to call themselves, have learned to live by a set of rules, by words spoken or printed, by a metaphysical system that would explain to them the very depth of human existence. Although it is difficult and even dangerous to speak of a national character and a collective mentality, it can be said in all fairness that the Germans are obsessed with the notion that there is always more to life and history than meets the eye. They are metaphysicists and mystics in spite of Immanuel Kant. It is no mere coincidence that in Goethe's *Faust,* their national poem, Mephistopheles, the "spirit who always negates," seduces Faust into the oblivion of sin. This is not merely the dramatic battle between good and evil in the "human breast," but the mirror of a world of black and white which has obsessed the German mentality. There is no performance of *Faust* in which

Mephistopheles, the Satan, is not depicted as a hook-nosed, black-haired, sly, shrewd, sophisticated creature. It is a carry-over from the Middle Ages, when the devil of mythology was identified with the Jews. Joshua Trachtenberg, an American rabbi, has devoted a scholastic book to this interesting phenomenon. I believe that it plays an important role in the specific brand of German anti-Semitism. It is not necessary, I hope, to say that I am aware of a host of creative German writers, of Thomas Mann and Hermann Hesse and many others, as indeed of thousands of Germans to whom this is not applicable. But the German masses have been susceptible to that kind of mystic anti-Semitism which we find nowhere else. After all, the fact remains that Germany is the only country in the world, the only people in all of history, who have translated anti-Semitism into unparalleled mass slaughter.

German anti-Semitism of the nineteenth century is the preface to the Nazi period. In terms of their anti-Semitic ideologies, the Nazis were imitators, the epigones of Wagner, Stoecker, Gobineau and Houston Stewart Chamberlain of the Bismarck era. Bismarck himself, who could have said with much justification that some of his best friends were Jews (the Jewish banker Bleichroeder was one of them), found it expedient to close his eyes and shut his ears. It suited his political battle against those socialists and liberals who opposed his conservative, dictatorial policies. Some of the leaders of the opposition parties were Jews.

Strangely enough, the theory of racial inequality was first advanced by a French nobleman, a diplomat and prolific writer, the Count Joseph Arthur de Gobineau. In addition to his famous volume on the Renaissance, he wrote a scholarly book called *Essai sur l'inégalité des races humaines*. It is, of course, not an anti-Semitic book, but it had a devastating anti-Semitic influence upon much of the thinking and action of that period. He claims that the notion of human equality is not borne out by the facts of history. Only the white races, he claims, are capable of creativity. And, above all, among the white races, it is the Aryan race which must be considered superior to all the others. It was left to the German racists to identify the Germans with "the Aryans." After this was done, the Germans became the only creative, indeed the super, race. Tragically, Friedrich Nietzsche added the philosophical touch that was needed. The *Will to Power*, the whole concept of the Superman, his contempt for weakness, the glorification of power, lust, strength, and even brutality lent respectability to the notion of German superiority. No wonder that Richard Wagner, who set the Germanic world of black and white, of good and evil, of Siegfried and Baldur to his glorious music, became one of the leading anti-Semites.

In fact, Wagner's world is the proper expression of this mystical German anti-Semitism. Christianity to him ought to have rejected the idea that "the God of our Savior had anything in common with the tribal God of Israel." He urged the Church to forsake the Old Testament, the Bible of those Jews "who are responsible for the decadence in culture, art and ethics." Wagner's son-in-law was destined to translate all this into a political theory which for a long time became the Bible of the German anti-Semitic racists. Houston Stewart Chamberlain, the son of an English father and a German mother, married Eva, Wagner's daughter. Among his admirers was Kaiser Wilhelm II, whose Pan-Germanic dreams brought Germany to its first disaster in 1918. Some serious Germans consider Chamberlain's book *Die Grundlagen des 19 Jahrhunderts* the "most impressive book written at the turn of the century." The book is an attempt to write European history based upon Gobineau's racial theory. European civilization, he claims, owes its greatness to the synthesis of the art of Greece, the law of Rome and the work of Christ. All these are "Aryan" creations, since Christ was a Galilean and "therefore an Aryan." The tragedy of the nineteenth century, he continues, lies in the fact that it has fallen prey to a racial mixture of people among whom the Jews are the lowest and most destructive. They are the classical and most dangerous enemies of the Ger-

manic and Christian spirit, and it is therefore impera-
tive that the European nations purify and rebuild the
Aryan race. This can be done only if Christianity
purges itself of the "Jewish" elements (Christ, the Aryan, did not want meekness but strength and courage)
and the German people rids itself of the destructive Jewish elements. The world is in the hands of
Jews, the racially impure descendants of Ignatius of
Loyola and the Pope. Thus the world is doomed.
There is but one cure for all the ills of the world: the
regeneration through the Aryan spirit, of which Germany is the purest expression, *Am deutschen Wesen
muss die Welt genesen* (Only the German spirit can
cure humanity).

Rubbish of this character was printed, read, applauded and accepted not by the masses, who did not
understand it, but by the elite of the German people,
particularly the academic teachers at the universities.
It would be worthwhile to make a thorough study of
the role of the universities in all the political upheavals of the last century and in our own time. Far
from being isolated in the ivory tower of learning and
scholastic investigation, both students and professors
participated as partisans during the political turning
points in modern history. Many German universities
were hotbeds of Nazism. I shall never forget that
night in a Berlin prison in 1933 when I discovered
that the black-uniformed SS officer who went from

prisoner to prisoner to beat him brutally was a class-
mate of mine at the University of Berlin and a Ph.D.
summa cum laude. It shattered many of my illusions
about the influence of philosophy upon human character and conduct. There were many highly educated
men among the leading anti-Semites of the Bismarck
era. Heinrich von Treitschke, head of the Department
of History at the University of Berlin, was one of them.
He was one of many political professors who gave respectability and professorial dignity to the anti-Semitic
movement. Treitschke, one of the spellbinders of his
time, based his historic-political theories on the superiority of the Aryan-Christian race and on the notion that "politics is power." He deserted liberalism in
1866 and followed Bismarck into the glorious era of
German victory over France and the creation of the
German Reich. To him Protestantism was the most
Germanic form of Christianity. He, too, would have
liked to see a church without Jewish heritage.

Protestant Christianity was to play a tragic role in
the development of German anti-Semitism even under the Hitler regime. William Shirer, a Protestant
himself, has attempted to trace this fact to Martin
Luther, who "was both a passionate anti-Semite and
a ferocious believer in absolute obedience to political
authority." Luther wanted Germany rid of the Jews,
and he advised that when they were sent away, "they
be deprived of all their cash and jewels and silver

and gold and, furthermore, that their synagogues or schools be set on fire, that their houses be broken up and destroyed."* Whether or not Shirer is right, the fact remains that the German Protestant Church was deeply involved in the politics of the Reich. The Kaiser was not only the commander-in-chief of the armed forces but also the head of the Protestant Church. The Church had an official position in the Reich, and German nationalism was deeply rooted in the Protestant Church and vice versa. An analysis of the German Protestant hymnal would reveal this mutual relationship. The church as well as the state was confronted with the growing social unrest among the workers. The liberal and socialist parties had fought for the rights of the laborers, and trade unions were being formed. The Church of Germany resorted to a device which had been tried in England in the first quarter of the century, the formation of a Christian-Social Workers' party. It claimed to combine Christian convictions with social gains and aspirations. Only through such a movement, they said, could the German workers be prevented from becoming atheists and traitors to the Reich. The founder of this movement, a member of the Reichstag, a chaplain at the Imperial Court, was Adolf Stoecker. It is interesting to note that Hitler's party was called the National Socialist

* William L. Shirer, *The Rise and Fall of the Third Reich*, p. 236.

German Workers' party. Only the word "Christian" was omitted. The ideology was the same.

Stoecker, who enjoyed the confidence of many persons in high offices, including the Kaiser himself, was a man of many talents. He was not merely a preacher and speaker of considerable ability, but a politician as well. In 1888 he was elected a member of the Reichstag. His party remained within the Conservative party but advanced its anti-Semitic program without any inhibition. Later, purely anti-Semitic parties with aggressive anti-Jewish platforms proved successful in elections. The first such deputy was elected to the Reichstag in 1887. But a few years later (in 1893) the number was increased to sixteen. Since the Conservatives approved heartily of anti-Semitic programs, the number of anti-Semitic members of the Reichstag was alarming. Stoecker was soon joined by Hermann Ahlwart, a man of much less reputation but of even greater demagogic talents. Ahlwart, a former schoolteacher who had been dismissed from the school system because of embezzlement of school funds, was assigned special duties. While Stoecker remained in the role of preacher and intellectual, Ahlwart attacked the Jews with unheard-of ruthlessness. In 1879 the Anti-Semitic League was founded. The word "anti-Semitism" had just then come into use. Ironically, it was coined by Wilhelm Marr, the son of a Jewish actor, who wrote one of the most violent anti-Jewish books. The league held its first international convention in Dresden and adopted as its platform "the liberation of the German Fatherland from complete Judaization and the preservation of conditions which will render the life of the indigenous German population tolerable." A more inaccurate description of the real situation was hardly possible. The Jewish population at that time was below 1 per cent of the German population, and the Germans were hardly in need of protection against them. Nevertheless, the economic difficulties for the middle class which had begun with the famous Black Friday of 1873, the world-wide crash at the stock exchange, made the Jews an easy target. The strange, incongruous mixture of rabble-rousers, university professors and ruthless politicians made the anti-Semitic Ahlwart-Stoecker movement a potent, dangerous German phenomenon.

There were similar movements in Austria. The political dilemma of the Jews was inevitable. They could not possibly be expected to back those reactionary political movements which were opposed to Jewish emancipation, and which demanded their exclusion from public offices and any other kind of influence. By conviction and in the interest of their self-preservation, they were liberals; some of them played important roles in these movements. To refrain from any political activities would have been an admission of defeat and a cowardly withdrawal from the struggle for full equality. It would also have been futile. The reactionary parties, on the other hand, took full advantage of this dilemma. Under the leadership of Karl Lueger, the mayor of Vienna, the anti-Semitic movement began to flourish. Soon the anti-Semites sent delegates into the Austrian Parliament. In the Nether-Austrian Parliament they commanded almost a majority. Although, unlike Germany, they found no encouragement from the Emperor, the Catholic clergy was only too eager to help. As Stoecker found Ahlwart to stir up the masses, so did Lueger find a mechanic by the name of Schneider who did the rougher jobs involved in arousing "the people's spontaneous anger." The material for the anti-Semitic campaign was supplied by the German movement. It was augmented by a professor of theology, August Rohling, who disregarded both truth and scholastic integrity when he published the anti-Semitic pamphlet *The Talmud Jew*. In this booklet, which was distributed by the thousands, he attacked not merely the Jewish people but the Jewish religion as cruel and primitive, implying that it is a religious duty of the Jew to attack Christians physically and that ritual murder (the extraction of blood from the bodies of Christian children) is a Jewish religious law. At a trial instigated by Dr. Joseph Bloch, a member of Parliament and a rabbi, he was accused of perjury and confronted with the testimony of leading Christian scholars, who charged him with ignorance and outright forgery. In the eyes of scholars and civilization he stood condemned. As usual, this had no effect upon the anti-Semites. Rohling's booklet is to this very day an anti-Semitic classic.

The greatest blow to the dream of equality for the Jews came from France. Here Emancipation had made great strides. From the very beginning the Jews of France had become part of the French people. The fact that physiognomically the Jews were not different from the French helped in the process of amalgamation. There could be no racial argument. It was evident that the black-haired Frenchmen were no "Aryans." In spite of their compatriot Gobineau, the French were contributing nobly to the creativity of the nineteenth century. This was the era of Pasteur in medicine, and in painting the great period of Degas, Pissarro, Manet, Toulouse-Lautrec and the other Impressionists. There was no reason for any sense of inferiority on that score. The national pride had been hurt by the crushing defeat of 1871. But the events which interest us here took place some twenty-five years later. They could not possibly be construed as a reaction to military defeat. The events, which became known as *L'Affaire* and which were to have more enduring consequence for France than either Stoecker had for Germany or Lueger for Austria, took place in 1894. They centered around a captain of the French army, the son of a well-to-do Jewish merchant, and himself a peripheral, "assimilated" Jew who had been attached to the general staff of the French army. The "Affair of Alfred Dreyfus" was to divide France deeply into "Dreyfusards" and "anti-Dreyfusards." It was destined to become the *cause célèbre* of Europe and one of the most fantastic phenomena in the long and protracted struggle for Jewish equality. It was also the most dramatic. Hannah Ahrendt in her *Origins of Totalitarianism* has analyzed both the "Affair" and the role of the Jew in the society of the nineteenth century, particularly in France. Nobody has made a more penetrating and fascinating study of the consequences of the Emancipation in terms of modern anti-Semitism. And none understands the Dreyfus Affair better. Her analysis should be read by those who wish to understand the Jewish problem in the framework of the development of the modern state. In the context of this book it must suffice to record the facts.

On October 14, 1894, Alfred Dreyfus, a captain of the French Army, was arrested on suspicion of high treason. Dreyfus was neither liked nor likable. He was the only Jew assigned to the general staff and thus had a difficult position, to begin with. His difficulties were aggravated by his constant bragging about his family's large fortune, his lavishness and his self-assertion. When it became known that a *bordereau* had been found in the wastepaper basket of the German Embassy, it was immediately assumed that the traitor could be no other than Dreyfus. The *bordereau* contained several secret documents addressed to Colonel von Schwarzkoppen, the German military attaché in Paris. The examination of handwriting was entrusted to Bertillon, who was not an expert in this field, but merely a criminologist. The trial was held in camera. It was carefully prepared by Édouard Drumont's *Parole Libre*, the leading anti-Semitic newspaper in France. The trial, held in December, took on Kafkaesque proportions. The defense was left completely in the dark. Although the accusation against Dreyfus was "documented" by a number of other pieces of "evidence" submitted by the anti-Semitic clique of generals, the defense was not informed of it. The verdict was swift and devastating. Dreyfus was convicted of high treason and sentenced to spend the rest of his life on Devil's Island off the coast of French Guiana. He was thirty-five years old. A few days later he was publicly degraded. Theodor Herzl, then a correspondent in Paris, gave an account of the event in the *Neue Freie Presse,* the leading liberal newspaper of Vienna:

Many curious people assembled on this cloudy winter morning in the vicinity of the Military Academy, not far from the building where the Exhibition of 1889 took place, to witness the formal degradation of Alfred Dreyfus. There were many officers in

uniform, most of them with their ladies. Only officers
and some journalists were permitted to enter the
court of the École Militaire. Outside was the multitude, usually assembled to witness an execution.
There were a large number of policemen. At nine
o'clock the huge courtyard was filled with soldiers,
altogether five thousand of them. In the center of the
square was a general on horseback. A few minutes
past nine, Dreyfus came out. He wore his captain's
uniform. Four men escorted him to the general. He
said: "Alfred Dreyfus, you are not worthy to wear
the uniform. In the name of the French people, I
herewith degrade you. The verdict will now be carried out." Then Dreyfus raised his right arm and
said: "I swear and declare solemnly that you are
about to degrade an innocent man. Vive la France!"
At this very moment there was the sound of drums.
An official of the court tore the buttons and epau-
lettes from the uniform. Dreyfus remained calm.
After a few minutes it was all over.

Now he was led toward the soldiers. He passed by
them like a man convinced of his innocence. When
he passed a group of officers they cried: "Judas!
Traitor!" Dreyfus replied: "I forbid you to insult
me." At twenty minutes past nine, this parade before
the troops was finished. Dreyfus was then handcuffed
and the police took over. From now on he was under the jurisdiction of the criminal courts. After he
was led away the soldiers began to leave in formation. But the mob closed in to watch every detail. "If
you let him out," they cried, "we'll tear him limb
from limb." But they waited in vain. The witnesses of

the public degradation left in embarrassed excitement. The firm attitude of the degraded man had left a deep impression upon some of them.

Four years later, remembering this "cloudy winter morning," Herzl reminisced:

> The affair of Dreyfus was more than a miscarriage of justice. It expressed the desire of a large majority of the French people to condemn a Jew and with him all of Jewry. À mort les juifs, shouted the mob, when they tore the epaulettes from his uniform. Where did all this happen? In France, in the modern, civilized republic of France, one hundred years after the proclamation of human rights. The people, or at least a considerable part of it, no longer want human rights for Jews. This is the repeal of the great revolution.

The issue was not merely anti-Semitism. Again, as always, the Jews were caught in an inevitable dilemma. It was the state which had given them rights. It was the state which permitted them to play their economic and social role. This state was an embattled republic. The military and the clergy, together with the Royalists, were eager to restore the Republic to the House of Bourbon. The Jews, deeply identified with the Republic, a Republic which had called the Jew Adolphe Crémieux to serve as Minister of Justice in a French Cabinet, were caught in the middle.

France was in reality a good illustration of the limitations of Emancipation in the nineteenth century. The amalgamation of the Jews into the body politic was quite imperfect. They had transferred themselves economically from the Middle Ages into the modern state. The "amalgamation" took place only on the same economic levels which had existed before; only their legal status had changed. But no change in their actual structure took place. There were no Jewish counterparts to every layer or even most layers of the non-Jewish population. The Jewish occupational structure remained unchanged. In a population where the peasant stock and the farmland still played an enormous role, this Jewish structure must have been considered "abnormal." It was on the level of the farm, in the villages, in the village inn, on the village green that the people expressed themselves in the genuine terms of their national life. The folk songs, the fairy tales, the anecdotes, the regional dishes — they all came from the village. The Jews had no part in it. Living in the urban centers, they participated in urban life on a higher economic level and with much more freedom than in the ghetto. But it was a transfer from the ghetto nevertheless. There were but a few Jewish doctors in the Middle Ages. Now there were many. There were moneylenders in the ghetto; now they were bankers. (The court Jews who had played a decisive part in the history of the eighteenth century were now leading and important figures in the financial community.) In the ghetto many Jews accumulated an assorted stock of merchandise left as collateral by the borrowers. Now they had department stores. Of course, some new professions were added, but not too many and none of them on the farm and in the village community. This was not merely a French problem; it was the heart of the problem of Emancipation. These, too, are the limitations of "assimilation." Only a few were socially accepted.

In her book on totalitarianism, Hannah Ahrendt examines those Jews who are "socially accepted." To her, it is the acceptance of the witty, the picturesque, the extraordinary. The Jew who is socially accepted is the one who least resembles the "normal" citizen. The bourgeoisie, successful and bored with success, needs entertainment. They need the colorful and exotic. The Jew provides both. The most outstanding example is Benjamin Disraeli, who began his fantastic career by emphasizing his Jewish physiognomy, wearing the most outrageous clothes, and gesticulating in the Oriental manner to such an extent that he shocked the members of the House of Commons after they had listened to his maiden speech. He never once ceased to stress his Jewish origin, which lent him dignity and nobility far superior to that of the English aristocracy. In today's post-Hitler Germany, many are displeased that the Jews have left Germany. They miss the "stimulating irritation" which came from Jewish writers, artists, playwrights and critics. "How can you live without salt and pepper?" the Germans ask. During a public debate with Paul Tillich on the Jews of Germany, I asked him whether he would advise Jews to return after Hitler's defeat. He replied: "Some of them should. Germany needs them. They have an important function: They are Germany's yeast." Thus the Jews had to think of themselves as the condiments of an otherwise spiceless society.

The Emancipation of the Jews brought considerable gains: citizenship, general education, a new self-respect, freedom of movement, the elimination of the ghetto prison, the rethinking of Jewish values, the creation of Jewish communities, the participation in literature, art and science. Yet there were danger zones and evidently a great deal of unfinished business. Anti-Semitism had become rampant in countries of diverse background: in Russia, in Germany, in Austria and in France. The countries had little more in common than the hatred of the Jews. It was an alarming setback of that great surge toward freedom and equality which had engaged the best minds and the most alert hearts in Europe since the days of the French Revolution. The last decade of the nineteenth century seemed to pose the question anew. It raised new doubts, new fears and, perhaps, some new hopes.

Beyond Nightmare and Dream

ALTHOUGH EMANCIPATION HAD PROVED a failure, the vast majority of the Jews in the Western countries, particularly the leaders who owed their positions to either their wealth or their religious authority, considered the affair of Dreyfus and the anti-Semitic movements mere episodes. They were not even ready to accept the Hitler regime as the beginning of the final liquidation of the Jewish communities. Since their views were based upon the rational optimism of the nineteenth century, which conceived of history as an irrevocable and irresistible chain of progress, they were unable to accept realities. To them anti-Semitism meant the "return to the Middle Ages" nurtured in the masses by depressions and ignorance. Their remedies for this malaise of society was "enlightenment" of the masses about the "true nature" of Judaism. They remained rationalists while the whole world had become emotional and nationalistic. They clung to their optimism when all signs of the time pointed to impending catastrophes. They had become prisoners of their own hopes and illusions. Thus the leading Jewish organizations in Germany, France and Austria preached this gospel of trust in mankind's goodness. Their main goal was to secure the rights of the Jews in their countries by emphasizing their patriotism, exalting the Jewish contribution to civilization, imploring the Jews of their constituencies to behave, not to become too conspicuous in the public affairs of the state and to wait patiently until, at last, the nations of the world would see the light and toleration would yield to acceptance. In spite of their money and influence, history swept them away, and many of these optimists died in the gas chambers of Auschwitz and Treblinka.

The forces which determined Jewish history remained a small minority, at least in the Western countries. They represented a new group in Jewish life, the products of assimilation and emancipation, and the severest critics of both. Zionism, which proved to be this history-making movement, is the result of the nationalist as well as emancipatory movements which dominated the century and without which the Zionist movement could not have come into being.

The new leaders of the Jews, who usurped the role formerly played by the descendants of the moneyed court Jews, were intellectuals rather than businessmen. Zionism is the reaction of the Jewish intellectuals to the failure of Emancipation. Even in Russia these intellectuals were postassimilatory Jews. It was by virtue of their "assimilation" that they were able to analyze and understand the Jewish situation in new terms. Unlike the Jewish bankers and businessmen, they did not have to defend and secure their economic positions. They had found their niche in the general community as writers, journalists, professors, physicians and lawyers. The little people who formed the bulk of the movement in Eastern Europe had nothing to defend anyway. The vested interests remained outside the movement. With Zionism, the secular Jewish intellectual assumes the role of leadership which he had never had before. Obviously, the religious leaders had nothing to offer. This rebellion of the intellectuals represents a significant change in Jewish life. Thus the first president of the Zionist movement was a newspaperman, and the last — before the creation of the state — a chemist. None of the "big families," the powers in the communities, participated in the movement. They stayed outside either as onlookers or as formidable enemies. The rabbis, many of them dependent upon the influential families, sided against the movement. The liberal branch of the rabbinate was openly hostile and attacked the new movement violently. The German rabbis prevented the holding of the first Zionist Congress in Munich. The American Reform rabbis adopted resolutions which rejected Zionism with unmitigated violence. There were, of course, some exceptions. Stephen S. Wise in America was one of them. The traditional rabbis joined the movement only through the Orthodox religious branch of Zionism.

The intellectual reaction to the bankruptcy of the Emancipation began in the middle of the nineteenth century; its first expression was from a German Jew, Moses Hess, son of a Jewish industrialist in Bonn. Hess, a close collaborator of Karl Marx and Friedrich Engels, developed his Jewish theory in *Rome and Jerusalem* (1862), which expressed his belief that the Jewish people would have to return to Palestine, the old homeland, in order to develop there the creative activity from which mankind would again benefit. The book hardly made an impression. The average Jew found it difficult to digest the Hegelian terminology with which the arguments were embellished. The majority of the spiritual and intellectual leadership rejected the ideas about a Jewish "race," which was one of the basic assumptions in the book. Only the historian Heinrich Graetz found some merits in it, and Theodor Herzl later praised it as the work of "the greatest Jewish philosopher since Spinoza." This was exaggerated praise. But it remains true that Hess anticipated much of the new national ideology: the concept of a Jewish nation, the idea of Palestine as a cultural center of the Jews and the hope for the revival of the Hebrew language.

Leon Pinsker, a Russian psychiatrist, was much more outspoken and his little book *Auto-Emancipation* much more influential. The title itself was provocative: *self*-emancipation was the prerequisite for collective emancipation. The pamphlet was first published in 1882, the year of the pogrom in Warsaw. Although it appeared in German, written by "a Russian Jew," it was widely read. When it became known that Dr. Leon Pinsker, a famous physician from Odessa, was the author, it attracted even more attention. Pinsker had been an assimilationist who had been active with those few emancipated Russian Jews who advocated complete Russification as the solution to the Jewish problem in Russia. The outbreaks of anti-Jewish riots in Russia converted him. *Auto-Emancipation* presents the first formulation of political Zionism. Written in the infancy of psychiatry, it applies psychiatric terminology and ideas to the Jewish problem. The Jews, after having lost their country, he said, are assumed to be dead. Yet they live among the nations. Thus they are a "ghost-like apparition." Anti-Semitism is the rejection of a ghost.

Along with a number of other subconscious ideas, instincts and idiosyncrasies [Pinsker writes], Judeophobia, too, has become rooted and naturalized among all the peoples of the earth with whom the Jews have had intercourse. Judeophobia is a form of demonopathy, with the distinction that the Jewish ghost has become known to the whole race of mankind, not merely to certain races, and that it is not disembodied like other ghosts, but is a being of flesh and blood, and suffers the most excruciating pain from the wounds inflicted upon it by the fearful mob who imagines it threatens them. Judeophobia is a psychic aberration. As a psychic aberration, it is hereditary; as a disease transmitted for two thousand years, it is incurable.

Of all the theories of anti-Semitism, it is probably the most profound, and as modern today as it was shocking in the nineteenth century. Pinsker's solution to the incurable disease of anti-Semitism is the removal of the ghost. The ghost people must return to its original form: a real people living on its own land, Palestine. The brochure was wildly greeted by the small groups of East European Jews who called themselves the "Lovers of Zion" (*Hoveve Zion*) and who advocated emigration to Palestine as the only solution to the Jewish question. The original "Zionists" had begun some settlements in the neglected little land that was then part of the bankrupt and corrupt Ottoman Empire. A small band of idealists, ill equipped and poorly trained, had begun to till the soil in the malaria-ridden land. Some colonies had been financed by Edmond de Rothschild, the famous Jewish benefactor of the century. Pinsker had provided the "scientific" theory. Soon he began to translate his theories into reality. Rejected by Western European Jews, he returned to Russia and worked with the small but dedicated groups of the Hoveve Zion, held convocations, planned emigration and failed. Toward the end of his life (he died in 1891) he realized that he had merely succeeded in creating a few colonies in Palestine maintained by philanthropy. Of the hundred famous Biluim, the first group of idealists, only sixteen had arrived in Palestine. It was a painful, small beginning. This, he understood, was not the solution of the Jewish problem.

The history of political Zionism begins with the emergence of a new leader in Jewish life: Theodor Herzl. His sudden preoccupation with Jewish affairs must have come as a shock to his colleagues at the *Neue Freie Presse* in Vienna, one of the great liberal newspapers of Europe, and even his own family. Herzl was not at all identified with Jewish "life." Nobody in his circle was. He was one of a group of assimilated, gifted young Jews who occupied many of the editorial chairs on large newspapers. Many influential European newspapers were owned by Jews in Berlin, Vienna and Paris. The Jews had developed a flair for writing in almost every field, but particularly in those columns which are known to European newspaper readers as *feuilletons*. Writing for these columns on matters political, literary or artistic required intelligence, inventiveness and wit. It was a style for which Heinrich Heine had set the tone. The writers of such *feuilletons* were often people of considerable literary ability, and many of them exerted great influence in a society in which the latest novel and the most recent theater performances were the topics of conversation both at home and in the sidewalk cafés. Herzl therefore was a well-known, much admired writer of short stories, plays and a book on French politics, *Le Palais Bourbon,* and one of the literary stars of the *Neue Freie Presse*. That this man, so thoroughly divorced from Jewish life, should emerge as a Jewish leader came as an almost appalling surprise to everybody who knew him.

Theodor Herzl was born in 1860 in Budapest into a Jewish middle-class family whose cultural milieu was German. Later he proudly traced his family to Spanish Jewish immigrants, but his Jewish background was limited. He received the usual superficial Jewish education, which consisted in reality of some preparation for his Bar Mitzvah, celebrated in accordance with Jewish tradition on the Sabbath following his thirteenth birthday. He hardly remembered the day. Nor did he remember anything that he had learned. Since the language used in the family was German, he did not know any Yiddish outside of the few words and phrases that had become part of the lingo of the coffeehouse literati of Vienna, where he and his family lived most of their lives. He, of course, knew no Hebrew. When, at the beginning of his public Jewish career, he passed through Sofia in Bulgaria, and was invited to attend Sabbath services, he stammered with trepidation through the Hebrew blessings which he had to recite. His knowledge of Jewish history and the great Jewish movements, books and ideas was so limited that very few references can be found in any of his writings. His favorite Jewish characters were the Maccabees because they fought for their freedom. Yet it would be a mistake to consider him a militarist. In his revolutionary plan for a Jewish State, he pleaded for political neutrality and for a small "professional army" to preserve order internally and externally. Nor was he familiar with many of the Jewish realities, either in the East or in the West. He knew of anti-Semitism from some personal experiences, but he grasped the problem of anti-Jewish prejudices as a symptom. He had a profound belief that the Jewish people would not succumb. A sense of honor and pride were his most outstanding character traits, and he wrote these sentences, which were founded on nothing more substantial than faith: "But the Jewish national distinctiveness neither can, will nor must be destroyed. It *cannot* be destroyed because the hatred of our enemies unites us. It *will not* be destroyed because we have proven it in the two thousand years of our appalling suffering. . . . Whole branches of Judaism might wither and fall. The tree itself will remain."

Such was the man who embarked upon one of the most fantastic adventures of our time. There is no doubt that he must be considered the most dominant and most influential figure in contemporary Jewish life. Without him we would have neither the State of

Israel nor the majority of those Jewish forces which have made the last half-century decades of Jewish revival and even renascence. Yet his public Jewish career lasted for but nine short, difficult, often heartbreaking years. It began in 1895, when he was a young, vigorous man of thirty-five, and it ended in 1904, when he died of a heart attack, weary, exhausted, and in the midst of some of the most violent battles in the Zionist movement, which he founded.

While in Anglo-Saxon countries political movements are created as part of the pragmatic process which faces practical problems and tackles them with political and other practical measures born of necessity, European political movements have their beginning in a book or even a pamphlet. The Socialist movement started with Karl Marx's *Das Kapital;* the movement of the anti-Dreyfusards and the renewal of France began with Émile Zola's *J'Accuse;* Communism received its great impulses from Lenin's writings; and the National Socialists based their political actions and ideologies on Hitler's *Mein Kampf.* So did the Zionist movement emerge after the publication of a slim volume: Theodor Herzl's *Der Judenstaat* (*The Jewish State*).

Der Judenstaat is relatively unknown today, and I doubt whether more than a handful of our contemporary Jews, let alone Christians, have ever read it. Yet, it is to this "pamphlet" (as Herzl himself was fond of calling it) that the whole Zionist ideology and movement owe their existence. Political books of this nature are prone to become the bibles of the movements which they create.

In his *Diaries,* published posthumously, Herzl describes his mood during the feverish days in Paris when the idea of the Jewish State suddenly took possession of him. He could hardly believe what he had written, and, in fact, the book was so completely out of tune with the thinking of the Western world that it is difficult to understand what actually had prompted him to write it. Many believe that the experience of the trial of Alfred Dreyfus, which he had attended as a reporter, must have made a profound impression on him. He himself rarely mentioned the trial in his *Diaries,* let alone considered this experience the moving force in his Zionist thinking. In reality, the Dreyfus affair was but one more (though probably the most glaring) symptom of what he called "the Jewish question." The Jewish question, that is, the existence of anti-Semitism in both social and violent forms, indicated to Herzl that the Emancipation was a dismal and catastrophic failure, and that assimilation was not the answer to the growing problem. This problem was — to him — of concern not merely to the Jews, but to the world at large. It must be considered a world problem, affecting the life of the Christian world as deeply as that of the Jews themselves.

The Jewish question still exists [he writes in *The Jewish State*]. It would be foolish to deny it. It was inherited from the Middle Ages, and civilized nations apparently are not able to get rid of it, however much they may try. They proved such generous desire when they emancipated us. The Jewish question exists wherever Jews live in appreciable numbers. Where it does not exist, it is being created through Jewish immigration. Naturally, we move to countries where we are not persecuted. But as soon as we arrive there, our very presence creates persecution. This is true of every country, and it will be that way even in highly civilized countries such as France until the Jewish question is solved on a political basis. Those unfortunate Jews are now transporting anti-Semitism into England. They have already introduced it into America.

In order to analyze the Jewish problem, a new approach to anti-Semitism must be found. It must be "understood" before it can be fought.

I believe [Herzl continues] that I understand anti-Semitism. It is, in reality, a highly complex movement. Of course, I look at it as a Jew, but neither with fear nor with hatred. I can discern many elements in it: vulgarity, ordinary jealousy of the competitor, inherited prejudice, religious intolerance, and even some completely fictitious defense mechanism. I believe that the Jewish question is neither social nor religious, although it sometimes assumes such forms. *It is a national question, pure and simple, which can*

only be solved by making it the national concern of
the world, a question which cries for international
discussion and an international solution.

These are some of the basic elements of Herzlian
thinking. This is a completely new concept. The Jewish problem is a world concern. When on November 29, 1947, I attended the historic session of the
Security Council which decided the creation of a Jewish State, I remembered the paragraph which I have
just quoted. The Jewish problem had finally come before the tribunal of the nations. Herzl was long dead.
But he was there, sitting invisibly behind every dele-
gate who had made the Jewish question the concern
of his government. By recalling the typical Jewish attitudes of the nineteenth century, it is easy to understand how revolutionary was Herzl's new approach.
Gone suddenly was the timidity. Gone also was the
fear to so much as pronounce the word "Jew" in the
presence of non-Jews. (How well do I remember my
father falling silent when we discussed things Jewish
around the table because the maid had come in to
serve the food.) Gone was any semblance of servility.
The back doors were closed forever. The Jewish question was no longer to be smuggled in, hushed up or
simply not discussed as though it were some incurable,
unmentionable malady. It is with this concept, which
lays the burden of discussion and solution upon the
shoulders of the statesmen of the world, that Zionism

begins. Even if it had not resulted in the creation of the Jewish State, it would have opened a radically new chapter in the relationship between the Jewish and the Christian worlds.

Behind this concept stood a man whose very appearance made this new approach believable. This was a new face in Jewish life. He was neither a successful businessman or banker (the usual president of a Jewish community) nor a saint or unworldly rabbi. The tall, elegant figure of the man with the beard of the nineteenth century, black mysteriously penetrating eyes and the firm voice of a born leader stood head and shoulders above the others. People who saw and heard him (and there are only a few such people left) would never forget him. He was indeed not merely a prophet, but also a king. When the cartoonists (particularly the Jewish caricaturists) mockingly called him "King Herzl," they admitted subconsciously that here at last was royalty, the spirit of Jeremiah and King David merging into one. It is unimportant whether a closer scrutiny of the man would justify such high-sounding and evidently exaggerated appraisal. But the belief in "objective" assessments overlooks the fact that the historic personality "makes" history through his legend. Herzl was a Jewish legend from the very beginning.

After defining the Jewish question as an international problem, he made a proclamation which fell like a bomb into the Jewish communities of the world: *"Wir sind ein Volk — EIN Volk"* (*"We are a people — ONE people"*). This idea was to dominate the public Jewish debate from that day until the present. Today it forms the very core of a new Jewish credo. In 1895 it sounded like a battle cry. Here indeed was the nullification of the entire Western effort of Emancipation. "To the Jews as a nation — nothing" was the threatening promise of the French Revolution. It remained the basic element in Jewish thinking. All the industry of the nineteenth-century Jewish leadership had been spent on the proof that indeed they were *not* a people but a faith, pure and simple. We were Englishmen, Frenchmen and Germans worshiping God in synagogues instead of churches. The notion of being a people (the German word *Volk* is much more definitive and closer in meaning to the English word "nation" than to "people") seemed not merely repugnant to the majority of West European Jewry, but a dangerous weapon in the hands of anti-Semites, who were looking for arguments against Jewish equality.

In the East European countries there was no stir about the first part of the proclamation. That the Jews are a people was taken for granted. In fact, it was a statement of the East European reality. What else were they but a people in Poland, in Russia and in Romania? They even spoke their own language, Yiddish.

They had created and enjoyed their secular culture, which they had developed in addition to their religious traditions. But the *second* part of the proclamation moved them deeply. For the first time a Jew, assimilated and highly respected, a journalist and playwright of note, said, not in *Yiddish,* the language of the ghetto, but in German, the language of Western civilization: We are one people. One people. Complete solidarity. No longer do boundaries of language and countries separate us. One people, because fate unites us. One people, because more than fate, a common *destiny,* ties us together. The sense of having been forsaken and even rejected by these emancipated, assimilated brethren of theirs was suddenly removed. A Western Jew had dared to identify himself with all of the Jewish people. This accounts for the fact that Leon Pinsker's book *Auto-Emancipation,* in many respects a much more profound book than Herzl's *The Jewish State,* failed to create the Zionist movement. Herzl, who had never seen the book, admitted that had he read it, he would not have written his "pamphlet." It would have been a historic tragedy. The call had to come from the West. Only a Western Jew could speak with the authority of his personal experience of the tragedy of assimilation and the failure of Emancipation. It is about the failure, the bankruptcy of the policy of assimilation, that Herzl writes most bitingly:

We have honestly tried everywhere to merge ourselves in the social life of the nations among whom
we live, and to preserve merely the religious faith of
our fathers. They will not permit us to do so. In vain
are we loyal patriots, and at times we are even chauvinistic. In vain do we sacrifice life and property as
do our Christian fellow-citizens; in vain do we try to
enhance the fame of our native lands by contributing
to the sciences and the arts, or the national wealth
through trade and commerce. In countries where
we have lived for centuries, we are still considered
strangers, and the accusation often comes from those
whose ancestors had not even lived in these countries,
when the Jews already experienced great suffering.
But in these matters, it is the majority that determines who is a stranger and who is not. In fact, in
matters of inter-group relations, the question becomes one of might and not of right. . . . In our
world and for some time to come, might precedes
right. It is therefore useless for us to be good patriots.
So were the Huguenots, and yet they had to emigrate.
If they would only leave us in peace. *But I believe we
shall not be left in peace.*

With this last sentence, Herzl enters the area of political prophecy.

Religious prophecy flows from the mysterious powers of God's personal revelation to the prophet whom
He calls. Political prophecy is dared by those who
have discovered a "propelling force" of historic pro-

portions which renders prophetic prediction possible. It flows from a political system, a historic scheme which makes certain developments inevitable. Herzl's political genius lies in this discovery and its application to contemporary Jewish history. *He firmly believed in a further and progressive deterioration of the Jewish situation in the world.* I sometimes wonder to what extent Karl Marx's theory of the "deterioration of the proletariat" had influenced Herzl. He was anything but a Socialist. But the parallel is too exact to be a mere coincidence. This "propelling force" Herzl calls "Jewish misery" (*Judennot*).

This "Jewish misery" is not an accidental, temporary phenomenon. It is the permanent crisis of Jewish life, a crisis which endangers the physical existence of the Jew. This permanent emergency, which might subside in times of prosperity only to reappear at moments of political upheaval or economic depression, was the direct result of an emancipation which never materialized. The Jews continue to live as strangers, and even foreigners, among nations which play host to them, and are conscious of this role. Guests must behave. The host is in command and always at liberty to open the door and ask them to leave. It is Herzl who coined the term *Wirtsvolk* (host nation). This host-guest relationship is in itself interesting. That the guest should have to behave is a Teutonic concept. It would be foreign to Orientals, to whom a guest is

an honored person. It would be alien to any civilized person who would rather want to please his guest
than to make his stay unpleasant. But Herzl's analysis
does not address itself to a civil situation. These Jews
who are considered guests, Herzl points out, had
lived in those "host countries" for more than a thousand years. It did not matter. Emancipation remained
an empty declaration. Assimilation was rendered impossible. From such consideration of a permanently
uneasy relationship which may at any given moment
explode, there is no other escape than to remove the
cause of the irritation. Since the indigenous people
who form the majority in the country will stay where
they are, it is the Jews who must move. Thus emerges
"The Plan."

The whole plan [Herzl writes in *The Jewish State*]
is basically very simple, as it has to be, if all people
are to understand it. Let sovereignty be granted us
over some portion of the globe, sufficiently large to
meet our rightful national requirements. We will do
the rest. To create a State is neither ridiculous, nor
impossible. Have we ourselves not witnessed the
process in our own time, among nations, whose majority was not middle class as we are but much
poorer, less well educated and therefore weaker than
we are? The governments scourged by anti-Semitism
will be deeply interested in helping us to obtain sovereignty. The plan, though simple in design, is complicated in terms of execution. It is therefore neces-

sary to create two agencies: the Society of Jews and
the Jewish Company. The Jewish Company will be
the liquidating agent for the business interests of the
departing Jews. It will also organize trade and commerce in the new country.

This, then, is no longer merely ideology. Here is a
journalist who had never dealt with practical matters,
let alone affairs of state, embarking on a fantastic plan,
which must have sounded ludicrous to his contempo-
raries in the Western world. He was very much aware
of it. Who was he, a Viennese coffeehouse Jew, to
speak about sovereignty of a state and the complex
enterprise of transplanting a whole people from one
continent to another? It must be borne in mind
that Herzl spoke here of "a territory." When later
England offered him Uganda in Africa as a possible
"territory for the Jews," or even El Arish in the
Sinai desert, he was very eager to accept. He was obsessed with the idea of a sovereign state which would
become, to use a Churchillian phrase of 1922, "as
Jewish as England is English." He was also afraid that
he would not be taken seriously. At times he was worried that he might be suspected of being paid for his
work. At this moment he was interested in being as
concrete and as practical as possible. The plan therefore continues in such terms:

We must not conceive of the exodus as a sudden
one. It will be gradual, stretching over a period of

decades. The poorest will go first and cultivate the soil. They will build roads, bridges, railroads, telegraph installations, divert rivers, construct homes, all according to a preconceived plan. Their labor will create markets, and markets will attract more settlers — for everyone will go voluntarily, at his own expense and at his own risk.

It was concrete, but it was not practical at all. Nothing actually happened the way he planned it. But this was immaterial. The general political approach was much more important. It was decisive in the development of Zionism. It was proof of Herzl's uncanny political instinct and a direct consequence of his concept of the Jewish problem as a problem of international concern. He rejected any form of "backdoor policy," any kind of slow infiltration into the new country. In the years after the publication of *The Jewish State*, this was one of the major issues. East European Zionists were much more in favor of immediate emigration, which would create a *fait accompli*, a Jewish "presence" in the country, rather than protracted negotiations with governments. Herzl was adamant. To him Zionism was "the Jewish people on its way home." It was in reality a government in exile. This in itself is a unique and ingenious political concept. The Zionist movement, representing "the Jewish people," had to act as though it were a government. It had to negotiate with "other" governments on an equal footing. This concept proved crucial. Without it the State of Israel would not exist today. It constitutes the victory of Western political experience and training over Eastern fervor and emotions. The following section of "The Plan" must be understood in this light:

> Those Jews who agree with our State idea will rally around the Jewish Society. Thereby they will give it authority in the eyes of governments to consult and act on behalf of our people. The Society will be recognized, to use a term of international law, as a State-creating power. *In fact, such recognition will already mean the creation of the State. . . .* The Society of Jews will negotiate with those powers who own the land, but it will be done under the sponsorship of European powers, if they prove friendly to the plan. We are in a position to offer the present authorities enormous advantages, such as the assumption of part of their public debt, build new highways and many other things. The very creation of the Jewish State would benefit neighboring countries, since the cultivation of land increases the value of the land around it.

There is, of course, no precedence either in international law or in history for this kind of concept. The "state-creating power" is a new term. There has never been such "power." There have been governments-in-exile waiting for the auspicious moment to return to their country and build a new independent state. There are many examples in our own time of countries which were under foreign domination and where patriotic nationalistic groups fought from within until the country was able to proclaim its independence. But never in history has there been a people scattered all over the world, with no country of their own, constituting themselves as a quasi-government of a country which did not yet exist. When Herzl wrote this sentence, he was not even sure whether it was to be Palestine or Argentina. This makes his "legal" concept even more fantastic. But it did work. Neither the romance nor the ingenuity of this Zionist idea is today fully appreciated. As the Jews are a people *sui generis,* so is the story of the creation of the Jewish State without parallel in the annals of world history.

The last paragraphs of *The Jewish State* must be quoted in full. They have aroused the emotions, the pride, the will power of a people whose suffering caused them to cling to this new great hope, who again, as in the days of the ancient Egyptian slavery, needed to be led "from serfdom to freedom, from darkness into light," from certain death into promising new life. This was Herzl's "propelling force." It lived in the hearts of a degraded people. The appeal came from a new prophet: in his appearance, in his voice, in his missionary zeal, a true descendant of Isaiah, the prophet of national hope. These are the words, addressed to the Jewish people, which stirred them to action:

> Here you have it, Jews. Neither fiction nor fraud. Every man may convince himself of it, for everyone will bring to the new land his own personal Promised Land — one in his mind, the other in his strong arms, and another one in his property which he acquired.
>
> Now, all this might seem to require a long time. Even under the best of circumstances it might take many years before we can create the State. In the meantime, Jews in a thousand places will suffer insult, mortification, abuse, humiliation and even death. But no, as soon as we begin to execute our plan, anti-Semitism will cease at once and everywhere. For this is a peace treaty with the world. . . . And what glory awaits those who fight unselfishly for the cause.
>
> I believe that a new, marvellous breed of Jews will spring from the new land. The Maccabees will leap to life again. Let me repeat: The Jews who will it shall have their State. We shall, at long last, live as free men on our own soil, and in our own homes we shall die, peacefully. The world will be liberated by our freedom, enriched by our wealth, magnified by our greatness. And whatever we shall achieve there for our own good will redound mightily and beneficially to the good of all mankind.

In a later book, *Altneuland,* he was to write the great, stirring motto, again addressed to the Jews: "If you will it, it will not be a fairy tale."

It was far from being a fairy tale. To the Jews in the Pale of Settlement, the Messiah seemed to have come. The small groups of "Zionists," desperate about their failure, responded enthusiastically. The assimilationists in the West reacted with anger and violent condemnation. The next nine years of Herzl's life, during which he sacrificed his entire fortune and his health, were devoted to activities so feverish as to be obsessive. He neglected his family, his job, his friends, and concentrated his energies to a point of complete physical exhaustion to the organization of the movement, and to a diplomatic activity during which he acted as the unofficial ambassador of the Jewish people accredited to a Jewish State which was little more than a figment of his political imagination. Both tasks were undertaken simultaneously. Although he had to admit that he had met with little practical success, these years of frustration proved decisive for the development of the movement and the later creation of the Jewish State.

In August of 1897 there met in the city of Basel in Switzerland the first international convocation of the Jews, the Zionist Congress. Never in the eighteen hundred years of the dispersion of the Jews had such an international gathering taken place, and its importance cannot be overestimated. Today it is taken for granted that Jews meet with their fellow Jews from all over the world. International cooperation is one of the important tasks of twentieth-century Jewry. This would hardly be possible had it not been for that first Zionist Congress. One hundred and ninety-seven Jews met, coming from many countries of the world (the majority, of course, from Eastern Europe), Jews of every possible description: Orthodox and Reform, Ashkenazic and Sephardic, Eastern and Western. In 1897 this was considered a unique and historic achievement. That it was accomplished was due to the passion and zeal of Theodor Herzl and to the burning Jewish problem, which required immediate solution. None of the great Jewish families was represented. With the exception of Max Nordau, the French writer, nobody of international reputation participated.

It was Max Nordau who gave the clearest analysis of the Zionist aim, not Herzl. It remains one of the best expositions of the historic motivations of the new movement. More succinctly than anybody who spoke at the first Zionist Congress did he define Zionism as the new answer to the failure of Emancipation.

> The nations [he said] which emancipated the Jews have deluded themselves as to their own feelings. In order to produce its full effect, Emancipation should first have been realized in sentiment before it was proclaimed by law. But this was not the case. The history of the Jewish Emancipation is one of the most remarkable pages in the history of European thought. The Emancipation of the Jews was not the result of a conviction that grave injury had been done to a

people, that it had been shockingly treated, and that it was time to atone for the injustice of a thousand years: *it was solely the result of the geometrical mode of thought of French rationalism of the eighteenth century.* Without reference to sentiment or emotion this rationalism, operating with logic alone, laid down principles as axiomatic as those of mathematics; it insisted upon trying to introduce these creations of pure intellect into a world of reality. The Emancipation of the Jews was an example of the automatic application of the rationalistic method. The philosophy of Rousseau and the Encyclopedists has led up to the declaration of human rights. The strict logic of the men of the Great Revolution deduced Jewish Emancipation from this declaration. They formulated a logically correct syllogism: Every man is born with certain rights; the Jews are human beings; consequently the Jews by nature possess the rights of man. *In this manner the Emancipation was proclaimed in France, not out of fraternal feelings for the Jews, but because logic demanded it.* Popular sentiment indeed *rebelled,* but the philosophy of the Revolution *decreed* that principles must be placed above sentiment. May I be permitted to say something which implies no ingratitude: *The men of 1792 emancipated us for the sake of logic.*

Nowhere in the entire Zionist literature will one find a clearer exposition of the postemancipatory conclusions to which the intellectuals had come and which accounts for the disappointment and emptiness of a generation which had vested all its hopes in the liberating forces of the Revolution. The sense of sobriety and numbness that characterized the intellectually alert witnesses of pogroms and degrading anti-Semitic propaganda found little response in the pedantic, shallow promises of the assimilationists. What was needed was not resignation to the sad facts of life, or a tepid sermon on progress that was "sure to come" and reason that was "certain to win at long last" (such was the language of the assimilationists of the time), but something that promised action, that gave an intelligent, brave and new appraisal of history and, above all, that gave new meaning to Jewish existence in the last years of the century. Zionism provided all this: analysis, action and a new *raison d'être*. It was particularly important to Western Jewry. While in the East Jews still clung to Jewish tradition, spoke the language of the ghetto, maintained Jewish schools, were steeped in Jewish knowledge, Western Jewry lived on precariously little more than memory and a religious tradition which had been diluted beyond recognition. To this generation, which had left the religious discipline of their parent generation, Zionism offered a new secular asylum for the spiritually homeless Jews. It was indeed the first secular Jewish movement. In its basic ideas, although it claimed religious neutrality, it violated one of the oldest religious principles of Judaism: the patient expectation of the coming of the Messiah. Zionism was a rebellion against the attitude of waiting. It was a negation of the concept of the Messiah who, according to tradition, will come "soon, in our own days." It was evident that he had not come, certainly not for the Jews. Alfred Dreyfus was waiting for the Messiah on Devil's Island, and the victims of the Russian pogroms were waiting in their graves. "To hell with waiting and bowing" was the beginning of one of the early Zionist songs. To hell also with begging the nations, with kowtowing and bending the knee, to hell with toleration and meekness, to hell with the whole timidity of the ghetto generation. This was the mood of the new movement. It was a movement of the young, even though some of the men were graybeards. But Herzl was only thirty-seven in 1897; Martin Buber was not even twenty; and Richard Gottheil, one of the first American Zionists, was thirty-five. The movement found the greatest response among the students at the universities. The response was so enthusiastic (although the numbers of the enthusiasts, it must be remembered, were very small), not merely because the movement provided an answer to the problems of the generation, but because this answer was born of the contemporary spirit of the European world. Zionism was a European movement, not a new Jewish sect.

Zionism as a political movement must be understood as one of the many expressions of the nineteenth-century nationalism. Herzl is made of the stuff that motivated Cavour to unite Italy and Masaryk to create an independent Czechoslovakia. Of course, the Jewish situation was unique, and we have already made the point that we deal here with a curious, unparalleled situation of a people without land. But leaving these unique features aside, Zionism was a nationalistic movement, and the emergence of the State of Israel cannot be isolated from the emergence of some sixty new sovereign states in the first decade after the Second World War. It would have been unthinkable in any other century. The concept of the freedom of the individual, formulated during the French Revolution, was enlarged and enforced in the concept of the freedom of the national group. Zionism is in a very real sense a movement of independence not unlike the movements which led to the creation of so many new, free, sovereign African states. Nationalism is not a pretty word in the American language, but the fact remains that our world cannot be understood without acknowledging the enormous influence of nationalism in terms of both power and the development of civilizations. It has, to be sure, developed into the extreme, racist, diabolic forms of German National Socialism and the despotism of Communist nationalism. But it has also led to the creation of a national consciousness that makes for a rich harvest of political, technical and scientific achievements. Zionism has not been entirely free of nationalistic exaggerations, nor is Israel today free of chauvinism. But it has, on the whole, created a new Jewish consciousness which has made for a greater, more useful, and more enduring Jewish contribution within and outside of Israel than in the period of ghetto docility.

That Theodor Herzl understood, or at least felt, the nationalistic implications of the movement becomes evident during the short period of his life which he dedicated to tireless efforts toward Jewish national independence. If the Jewish people were to achieve national independence in a sovereign Jewish state, it was necessary to negotiate with the powers which would create the conditions under which such sovereignty was possible. The means, both financial and physical, as he knew and emphasized again and again, were to be provided by the Jews themselves.

Palestine was then a province of the Ottoman Empire, a country which suffered from the chronic diseases of corruption, illiteracy and lack of leadership. The Sultan Abdul-Hamid II was characterized by Bismarck as "that sick man at the Bosphorus." Yet it was the very sickness (lack of funds and an international supervision of Turkey's *dette publique*) that provided Herzl with the solution to his problem. His negotiations, if his conversations with the higher and lower echelons of the ruling court clique, and later with the Sultan himself, can be called that, were based upon a simple proposition: the Jewish people were to assume financial responsibility for part of Turkey's indebtedness. A sober investigation into this proposition would reveal how utterly fantastic the plan was. Herzl based it on rather superficial advice which he received in Vienna, and the audience with the Sultan was arranged by a Polish scoundrel, the Baron Newlinski. The journey to the Turkish capital and the court intrigues in which he was involved read like a political detective story. In spite of the fact that the Sultan was deeply impressed, nothing came of it. Herzl had asked for very little. All he wanted was a "charter" which would officially permit Jewish settlement in the area of Haifa bay. The idea of the charter was to dominate the Zionist discussion. Herzl was obsessed with international guarantees. Everything else seemed underhanded. East European Zionism never understood this obsession with the charter and began to call it "Charterism."

The discussions with the Sultan were not the only political action. Herzl's first political contact was with the liberal and generous Grand Duke Frederick of Baden. It was through him that one of Herzl's dreams came true, an audience with the German Kaiser Wilhelm II. That this should have been possible was in itself no mean achievement. Herzl had two purposes in mind. He wanted to enlist the Kaiser's help in influencing the Sultan, and secondly he wanted to interest the German government in sponsoring Jewish settlements in Palestine in case Germany should want to establish a zone of influence there. Plans for the famous Baghdad railroad were being discussed, and the Germans were eagerly looking toward establishing a German bridgehead in the Near East. The audience had been arranged with the help of the Grand Duke. The Kaiser received Herzl in Constantinople in October 1898, and then a few weeks later in Jerusalem during the Kaiser's stay in Palestine. Herzl, always deeply impressed by "real nobility," admired the Kaiser's very appearance. "When I came in," he writes in his *Diaries,* "the Kaiser looked at me grandly with his great sea-blue eyes. He has truly Imperial eyes. I have never seen such eyes. A remarkable, bold, inquisitive soul shows in them." The conversation began with a formal statement, which Herzl had to submit to Bernhard von Buelow, Secretary of Foreign Affairs, and later Chancellor of Germany. The Kaiser seemed mildly interested. Buelow was hostile from the very beginning. The Kaiser's blue eyes lit up only when he made some slightly anti-Semitic reference to Jewish wealth. "Money," he said, "you have plenty. Your people have more money than we." He agreed with Buelow that the Jews had proved themselves rather ungrateful to the imperial household "in spite of what His Majesty's father and grandfather had graciously done for the Jews." This was a reference to the role which some Jews played in the German liberal parties.

Herzl, at times ill at ease, but also conscious of the great honor of being in the presence of the mighty German Emperor, was realistic enough to sum up the result of these two interviews: "He said neither yes nor no." It was evident that Germany was not to be counted upon.

From the very first consideration of a concerted political plan, it was clear that the Christian Church could not be overlooked. This was particularly true of the Roman Catholic Church, and a visit to the Vatican was indicated. The preliminary conversation with the Secretary of State, Merry del Val, was not very encouraging. Pope Pius X, who had just ascended to the throne of Peter after the death of Leo XIII, confirmed this first impression. The account in the *Diaries* gives a fascinating description of the audience. The attitude of the Vatican has hardly changed to this day. The conversation was conducted in Italian. Herzl first apologized for his "miserable Italian." But the Pope said: *"No, parla molto bene, signor Commendatore."* He called him "Commander" because Herzl was wearing the medal which the Sultan had conferred upon him. Herzl had not kissed the Pope's hand, and he suffered from this omission of etiquette throughout the audience. "I believe that I incurred his displeasure by this, for everyone who visits him kneels down and at least kisses his hand." The Pope, "a good, coarse-grained village priest," was seated in an armchair and listened, slightly annoyed, to Herzl's request. Then he said "sternly and resolutely": "We cannot give approval to this movement. We cannot prevent Jews from going to Jerusalem — but we could never sanction it. The soil of Jerusalem, if it was not always sacred, has been sanctified by the life of Jesus Christ. As the head of the Church, I cannot tell you anything different. The Jews have not recognized our Lord, therefore we cannot recognize the Jewish people." There was little room for argument. The Pope repeated that if the Jews would come to Palestine "we shall have churches and priests ready to baptize you all."

Before going to the Vatican Herzl had seen Victor Emmanuel, the King of Italy. The account in the *Diaries* reads like the first act of an Italian comic opera. No promises were made. No action was proposed. The King was very optimistic about the Jewish State, very polite and completely noncommittal. The fact that a Jew, Luigi Luzzatti, was Prime Minister, and another Jew, Senator Malvano, was the actual head of the Foreign Office was another stumbling block. They preferred "to discuss only art and science with me," not Zionism. The most daring of all the political interventions was Herzl's visit to Russia and his interview with Vyacheslav Plehve, the Minister of the Interior, an archenemy of the Jewish people. It took place in August of 1903, the year of the pogrom

of Kishinev. It was the most criticized political nego-
tiation and the most typical of all. To see Plehve on
behalf of the Jewish people was like trying to convince
Hitler. It meant trading not merely with the enemy
but with Satan himself. No such considerations in-
timidated Herzl. If making a pact with the Devil was
to help solve the Jewish problem, it was his duty to do
so. He presented to Plehve a memorandum with a
threefold program: "First, effective intervention with
His Majesty the Sultan. Second, the Imperial Russian
Government would provide a financial subsidy for
emigration, using for this purpose certain funds and
taxes whose provenance is purely Jewish. Third, the
Imperial Russian Government would facilitate the
loyal organization of Russian Zionist societies according to the program of Basel."

The conversations with Plehve took place in an atmosphere of apprehension. The pogrom of Kishinev,
the bloodiest of all the pogroms, had aroused a storm
of protest against Russia. Public meetings in London
and in New York condemned Russian cruelty. Theo-
dore Roosevelt, the President of the United States,
had threatened to sever America's commerical relations with czarist Russia. The Jewish problem was
very real. Russia's interest in Jewish emigration was
to them a matter of self-preservation. At least that
part of the Zionist program would be supported by
Russia. They were worried, however, about the cul-

tural program of the Zionists, the socialist tendencies and the awakened national spirit among Zionists. This new trend might cause the Jews to stay in Russia, rather than leave for Palestine. But on the whole, the visit was successful. For Herzl it provided the first opportunity to meet Russian Jewry in its own setting. The reception was tumultuous. The Russian police stood by helplessly, watching thousands of Jews who greeted Herzl in Vilna as though he were the Messiah. "I had to avoid riding on a white donkey in order to prevent being mistaken for the Messiah." The assimilated Jew, accustomed to orderly, well-behaved, reasonable Jews, was suddenly confronted with uncontrolled mass emotion, an avalanche of hope born of desperation and expectations of a new freedom which reminded him of the Jewish slaves of ancient Egypt on the eve of their departure into freedom. He was moved to tears.

The Russian Zionists, who had watched Herzl with great admiration as he rose at the first Zionist Congress to proclaim a new Jewish liberty to the world, had by now become more reluctant with their praise. The gap between East and West had widened. Chaim Weizmann in his memoirs, *Trial and Error,* expressed this growing skepticism:

> Herzl's pursuit of great men, of princes and rulers, who were to "give" us Palestine was the pursuit of a mirage. It was accompanied, most unfortunately, but

perhaps inevitably, by a shift to the right. Herzl
played to the rich and powerful, to Jewish bankers
and financiers, to the Grand Duke of Baden, to
Kaiser Wilhelm II and to the Sultan of Turkey; later
to the British Foreign Secretary. We, on the other
hand, had little faith in the benevolence of the
mighty. . . . There was a more general revolt on
the part of the Russian Zionists against the Western
conception of Zionism which we felt to be lacking in
Jewishness, in warmth, and in understanding of the
Jewish masses. Herzl did not know Russian Jewry;
neither did the Westerners who joined him. . . .
They did not believe that Russian Jewry was capable
of furnishing leaders to the movement.

The open conflict with Herzl at the sixth Zionist
Congress in 1904 expressed in violent terms the deep
and genuine conflicts between Russian Jews, who had
lived through the hell of pogroms and ghettoization
and who were uncompromising in their demand for
a national home in Palestine and nowhere else, and
Western Jews, to whom the Jewish problem was a
political question to be solved by patient negotiations
and acceptance of political realities. Shortly after the
sixth Congress, Herzl died. He left the movement to
East European Jewish leadership. It was to have a
profound influence on the tone and mood of Zionism.
Herzl's successor, David Wolffsohn, though he lived in
Germany, was a Lithuanian Jew. The political legacy
of Herzl and his most far-reaching achievement, from

which his critic Weizmann and the movement were to benefit and which led to the Balfour Declaration, was Herzl's consistent political contacts with England.

The English people have shown a remarkable preoccupation with the historic role of the Jewish people. Since Oliver Cromwell readmitted Jews to England, there existed in England a readiness to solve the Jewish problem through their restoration to their old homeland, Palestine. The English voices among pre-Herzl Zionists are the most articulate, and they are all Christian. It is no coincidence that one of Herzl's earliest and most ardent followers was William Hechler, Protestant chaplain of the British Embassy in Vienna, who had written a pamphlet in 1882 titled *The Restoration of the Jews to Palestine According to the Prophets*. It was not an isolated event in the history of English thought on the subject. In some strange fashion the return of the Jews to Palestine was anchored in the ancient Christian movement of the millennium, which expected Christ to return to the earth in order to govern the world in righteousness. Since this reign was to right all wrongs, it was also to reestablish the ancient people of Israel on its own soil. Although such thoughts were strictly theological, they found some interesting expressions in certain political attitudes in England. We have already mentioned the fact that Benjamin Disraeli emphasized his Jewishness, his Oriental nobility of Israelitic origin, in his ambition for the highest political position. In England this was not only possible but applauded. At any rate, it proved successful. In Palestine itself, English voices were heard which advocated Jewish settlement long before Herzl. Some fifty years before the first Zionist Congress, Colonel Churchill, British Consul in Syria, suggested that the Jewish nation should be reestablished in the ancient homeland. In 1840 Lord Palmerston made a similar suggestion to the rulers of Turkey. It was part of his grandiose scheme of a regenerated Turkey protected by England and other powers against Russian ambitions. A Jewish Palestine fitted well into this plan. Much later Lord Arthur Balfour delivered a moving address at the dedication of the Hebrew University of Jerusalem and emphasized this profound, religious, Biblical and almost mystic bond between the English spirit and the dream of Israel rebuilt.

It is against this background that Herzl's successes in England must be evaluated. Although no practical action resulted from his negotiations, at least not in his lifetime, the discussions with the British government were of the greatest importance for the Zionist movement. They established for the first time that a people without land and power could negotiate with a well-established government and be taken seriously. We mentioned the plan to place El Arish, in the Sinai Peninsula, at the disposal of the Jewish people. The proposal was made by Lord Lansdowne, the Foreign Secretary, and accepted by Herzl because of its proximity to Palestine and as a first step toward final settlement there. A commission was sent out to study the land. It proved too arid for settlement. Joseph Chamberlain then suggested the uninhabited areas of the East Africa Protectorate and finally an area of six thousand square miles in Uganda. In the face of the growing urgency created by the untenable situation in Russia, Herzl was ready to accept. The Russian Zionists rejected the very idea of settlement outside of Palestine. Herzl's death eliminated him from further discussion. Some of his followers now formed a new movement of Territorialists, who were willing to accept any land for Jewish settlement. The movement was later used for anti-Zionist propaganda purposes, but it had distinguished adherents. The British plan was finally rejected and shelved. But England remained the great hope.

When the First World War began in 1914, the Zionist Organization had developed into a well-organized political machine with departments of agriculture, finance and politics. The practical infiltration into Palestine, now the agreed method of Zionism, had borne fruit. In 1914 the Jewish National Fund, which purchased land, owned property valued at £144,000. This was tremendous progress; in 1907 the value of their land was a mere £11,000. There were ninety thousand Jews in Palestine, thirteen thousand of whom were settlers in forty-three agricultural settlements. For purposes of political maneuverability, the headquarters of the Zionist Organization were moved to a neutral country, to Copenhagen in Denmark. By the beginning of the First World War the Zionist movement was less than two decades old, yet it had already become an important factor in Jewish life. To be sure, the program of emigration to Palestine was limited. The mass emigration was to America. In spite of all the national and religious sentiments, Russian Jews went to the United States, a country of unlimited possibilities, waiting for immigrants, promising freedom and bread at the very moment of need. Palestine, neglected, hot, dangerous and unhealthy, lured only the adventurous and the Zionist idealists. While a million East European Jews came to America in the wake of the Russian pogroms, only some thirty thousand had reached Palestine since 1881. While the numbers were most discouraging, the caliber of the people was not. The famous Russian second aliyah provided the political and military leadership of the State of Israel today. Men like Ben-Gurion, Sharett, Meir Dizengoff, founder and first mayor of Tel Aviv, and countless others came with that group. Weizmann himself, though he did not settle in Palestine, was of this generation. The fantastic story of the renascence of the Hebrew language as a modern tongue was written and lived by these Russian Jews. The concept of a new agricultural community based upon prophetic and modern concepts of social justice, which led to the establishment of the communal settlement (*kibbutz*), is the product of Russian-Jewish thinking under the guidance of A. D. Gordon. A new ethos of work, which forbade the employment of Arabs for menial labor and called upon the settlers to assume all responsibilities in the settlement and in the cities, was proclaimed. While the scale of such endeavors was minute, it was an important step toward self-government at a time when Jews would be the majority population. In 1914 this goal seemed to be so far off as to be Utopian. Ninety thousand Jews lived among more than six hundred thousand non-Jews. A Jewish State with a non-Jewish majority was an untenable proposition. No wonder Zionists thought that only their grandchildren might some day see the establishment of the Jewish State. Nobody had the faintest notion or any realistic plan that could work this miracle. They knew that for as long as they lived they would have to live with a dream.

But living with a dream was, strangely enough, what they needed most. Jewish life was either boring or bloody. Little was left in the Jewish life of the Western countries that was exciting. Even anti-Semitism had begun to subside. Jews in the Western world breathed much more freely now. The years between the turn of the century and the First World War looked like the beginning of a golden era. The Jews in Eastern Europe had begun to leave for countries abroad. But even to them a dream, however Utopian, was important. It is difficult to appreciate fully what Zionism meant to the Jews in terms of their own self-fulfillment. Suddenly new songs were on their lips. Jews in the West, who had never met East European Jews, discovered this new world through Zionism. Martin Buber interpreted Hassidism, the Podolian mystical movement of the eighteenth century, and told the stories of the Hassidic rabbis in marvelous modern German. He began to translate the Bible into a new "Hebraic" German. Assimilated German and French Jews began to study Hebrew. A whole new literature was written. Jewish publishing houses, magazines and newspapers interpreted the new ideas on the highest possible level. Suddenly it had become fashionable to read Sholem Aleichem and Pérez in a German or French translation. A Swiss university published a volume of collected Yiddish folk stories as a doctor's thesis and, for the first time, Yiddish appeared in a scientific transliteration. Jewish folk music was presented in the concert halls of the world. A new Jewish pride swelled the hearts of the children of the ghetto. The debate on the solution to the Jewish problem stimulated the thinking of the communities. The most radical of the Zionist thinkers, foremost among them the German-trained but Russian-born philosopher Jacob Klatzkin, predicted the doom of the Diaspora. Western Zionists, whose ancestors had lived in these countries for generations, started a Jewish revivalist movement with unheard-of fervor. Some of them, sons of families so assimilated that they had forsaken the ancient rite of circumcision, had themselves circumcised at the age of twenty-one. Most Western Zionists accepted Herzl's notion of the host-nation and no longer considered themselves Germans or Frenchmen, but simply Jews living, by accident of birth, in those countries. Some of the sons of the most peripheral Jews returned to Orthodoxy. All of them began to understand their own humanity in terms of their Jewishness. Zionism to them was to be the belief of the elite, and only the best should settle in Palestine. A model movement was striving for a model country. All human values were to be renewed in the new life. Youth movements, adopting the philosophy of the German school of "Youth Culture," enlisted thousands of young people and discovered nature for the Jewish people, so long and so wrongly concentrated in urban centers. Many of them changed their professions and proclaimed that a new occupational structure had to be created in the Diaspora in order to create a normal society in the new land. Jewish parents still dreamed of the son who someday would be a successful and honored doctor. The son, however, prepared himself to become a first-rate cabinetmaker. A new idealism, naïve and wonderfully unrealistic, had taken hold of the young Zionists. All this was accomplished by a new dream. How good, how perfectly marvelous, it was to live with a dream. Rarely had a nationalism been channeled into such ideas of human grandeur and nobility. The dream was fed by the best in literature and art. It was not a ghetto dream. Even the Zionist youth movements of Eastern Europe became part of this new renaissance. Political socialism very often yielded to religious, or at least ethical, ideas of justice for all. The most stringent laws of purity in their personal lives were imposed upon this elite. That the numbers of these groups were actually very small only heightened their sense of nobility.

The war was to bring radical changes. Dramatically and as though driven by invisible forces, the Zionist dream came closer to fulfillment than ever before. Zionism seemed to offer a solution not merely of the Jewish problems, but of a world problem as well. Turkey, which played a pivotal part in the fight for the possession of Palestine, sided with Germany. In case of victory, the fate of the Ottoman Empire was in the hands of England. And there was no doubt that the Allied forces would win. An unexpected turning point was reached. On November 2, 1917, a letter was sent to Lord Lionel Walter Rothschild. It was a brief note written on the stationery of the British Foreign Office. The text was to become one of the most widely discussed and interpreted political documents of our time:

DEAR LORD ROTHSCHILD,

I have much pleasure in conveying to you, on behalf of His Majesty's Government, the following declaration of sympathy with Zionist aspirations which has been submitted to, and approved by, the cabinet. His Majesty's Government views with favor the establishment in Palestine of a national home for the Jewish people and will use their best endeavors to facilitate the achievement of this object, it being clearly understood that nothing shall be done which may prejudice the civil and religious rights of existing non-Jewish communities in Palestine, or the rights and political status enjoyed by Jews in any other country. I should be grateful to you if you would bring this declaration to the knowledge of the Zionist Federation.

Yours,
ARTHUR JAMES BALFOUR

The Balfour Declaration was the result of a combination of political negotiations and the world situation in the last year of the war. The political negotiations had begun with Herzl's attempt to interest the British government in the idea of the Jewish State. When, in 1903, the government offered Uganda to Herzl, it was considered the first political success of the young movement. Although the project was not accepted by the Zionists, it indicated for the first time that the Zionist plan, rejected as fantastic and even dangerous by the assimilated Jews, was taken seriously by one of the great powers of the world. It is important to remember that the name of the Prime Minister whose government had offered Uganda to the Jews was Arthur James Balfour. A year later, a young Russian chemist, a severe critic of Herzl's charter policy, moved to England. His name was Chaim Weizmann. It was his fate that he was to vindicate Herzl's political Zionism, which called for patient perseverance and slow, painful negotiations in the face of violent and impatient criticism on the part of Zionist activists. Herzl's tragedy repeated itself in Weizmann's biography. Weizmann's early contacts in England were with Balfour himself, who showed an early interest in a Jewish Palestine. There were others. Cyril P. Scott, the distinguished editor of the *Manchester Guardian,* introduced Weizmann to Herbert Samuel, then a member of the Cabinet and later the First High Commissioner in Palestine under the British mandate. Samuel believed that the disintegration of the Ottoman Empire might afford an "opportunity for the fulfillment of the ancient aspiration of the Jewish people and the restoration there of a Jewish State." He found understanding among his political colleagues and friends as early as 1914, notably David Lloyd George and Sir Edward Grey. A memorandum with a more detailed plan was submitted to the Cabinet early in 1915. In the same year the *Manchester Guardian* published a leading editorial which called for the creation of a buffer state in Palestine for the protection of Egypt and the Suez Canal. The article claimed that only a Jewish State would provide the protection by a people who would be a reliable ally of Great Britain, bound by bonds of gratitude for the establishment of a Jewish State.

The English Zionists, who were mostly Manchester men (Weizmann taught at the University of Manchester), were men of influence in public life: Harry Sacher, then a correspondent of the *Manchester Guardian,* Israel Sieff and Simon Marks (now the heads of one of the leading merchandising firms in Great Britain) and a host of sympathizers, among them members of the influential Rothschild family. American Zionists had just at that time become an active political group. Under the leadership of Louis D. Brandeis, since 1916 a Justice of the United States Supreme Court, a small but extraordinary group of people formed the Zionist Cabinet: the young preacher Stephen S. Wise, consumed with the prophetic idea of justice; Louis Lipsky, the most eloquent and articulate interpreter of Zionist ideology; Judah

Leon Magnes, one of the first Zionist Reform rabbis of America and one of the purest idealists of American Jewry.

The political constellation during the First World War which gave birth to the Balfour Declaration had some interesting Jewish aspects. The archenemy of the Jews, Russia, was one of the Allies. It was only natural for the Jews in neutral countries (and America remained neutral until 1917) to side with the Germans. Indeed, the German armies occupying Russia were wildly greeted by the Russian Jews. Fantastic though it may seem today, the Germans were the liberators of the ghettos. The Kaiser, himself an anti-Semite, ordered his generals to issue a proclamation in Yiddish to the liberated Polish Jews which bore the famous salutation: *"Tzu meine lieben Yidden"* ("To my beloved Jews"). In Germany proper, the government was eager to please the Jews, and German Zionists submitted serious memoranda calling for a Jewish Palestine under a German protectorate. The Allies, and particularly England, were eager to please the Jews. A pro-German attitude of American Jews, for instance, could influence the American government to withhold assistance from the Allied cause. The future of the Near East alarmed British political circles. There were serious claims on the part of France, particularly in Syria, of which Palestine was considered a part. A secret treaty between England and France, known under the names of the two negotiators of the agreement as the Sykes-Picot Treaty, had already promised much of Palestine to France and recommended that the rest be placed under international supervision. There were other plans which called for some kind of partnership between several nations, notably France and England, in the administration of Palestine after the war.

It was at this moment that the Zionist Organization submitted a document to the Imperial War Cabinet which formed the foundation of the Balfour Declaration. The document is interesting, but it is unnecessary to quote it here since it contains all the Zionist demands which had been made since Herzl. What is more interesting is Chaim Weizmann's self-analytical observation. It speaks well of the man's humanity and greatness. As the leader of a movement, admired as a diplomat and world-renowned biochemist, he was still capable of smiling at himself in humble amazement. This is what he writes in his memoirs as a footnote to the document presented to the Cabinet of the most powerful empire of that time:

> It [the document] represents the efforts of a group of amateur state builders, members of a people which had for many centuries been separated from this type of activity. None of us had any experience in government and colonization. We had no staff of experts to lean on, no tradition of administration, no civil serv-

ice, no means of taxation, no national body of land
workers. We were journalists, scientists, lawyers,
merchants, philosophers. We were one or two generations — if that — removed from the Ghetto.*

This is the romance of Zionism and the miracle of the
State of Israel. After all, the people who accomplished
the miracle were sons of secondhand dealers and peddlers. It might well be that such philosophical observations call for a reevaluation of the importance of ex-
perts and tradition in the field of political planning
and achievement. It might also be true that those
trained for the task of building states and diplomatic
negotiations could not have achieved what these ama-
teurs accomplished.

The American political scene unfolded the amazing phenomenon of a professor-president, Woodrow
Wilson, who projected a new America in 1917, to
the embarrassment of the isolationists and provincials,
who still dominated political life. His "Fourteen
Points," which captured the imagination of the liberal
world for some time, foretold of an America deeply
concerned with the fate of the weak and unprotected,
bent upon freedom for all, and particularly for the
fettered nations, small or large. It had Messianic
scope. It projected the American Declaration of Independence against the world screen and had the
ethical ring of great political documents. "Self-

* Chaim Weizmann, *Trial and Error,* p. 186.

determination for the peoples under Turkish rule," "independence of Poland," the "formation of a general association of nations . . . for the purpose of . . . political independence and territorial integrity to great and small states." This is the language of the twentieth century! This is the prelude to San Francisco of 1945. This is the dream and fulfillment of the post-Second World War era. It spelled freedom for Czechoslovakia and Armenia. It promised protection for national minorities. It also created a new political and ideological climate for the creation of the Jewish State. The Balfour Declaration, diluted as it was and speaking of a Jewish national home *"in* Palestine" instead of Palestine *as* the national home, was a great victory for the Zionist movement. It was — thirteen years after his death — the vindication of Herzl's "Charterism." It was, indeed, The Charter. Only it was not guaranteed by a corrupt Turkey; it was safeguarded by England.

The document, which underwent many changes before it had been reduced to the few sentences in Balfour's famous letter, was to become a bone of much contention to the military and political leaders of England in the years to come, and some people called it an irresponsible and even lunatic act on the part of Great Britain. So many other commitments had been made to the Arabs that Palestine was to be called the "much too often Promised Land." It is therefore of interest to quote Weizmann's observations which he made to one of the Zionist Congresses of that time: "England with its world-embracing view understood sooner and more fully than any other nation that the Jewish problem lies like a shadow over the world and can become a tremendous force either for construction or destruction. That is why it was not the English *generals* but the English *intellectuals* who were directing the foundation of our policy." This is an interesting comment on the part of the leader of a movement which itself was a movement of intellectuals rather than practical, hard-boiled, calculating businessmen.

The year 1917 coincided with another important event in human history which had, of course, world-shaking consequences. It also had important bearing upon the fate of the Jews. The czarist regime of Russia was overthrown by a revolution and the Kerenski government came into being, proclaiming freedom and equality for all peoples living in Russia. Thus 1917 became the year of the Emancipation of the Russian Jews. Since nobody foresaw the consequences of a Communist tyranny for either Russia, the world or the Jews, the event was greeted with enthusiasm by the whole world, and the Jews hailed it in terms of a new deliverance of their people from another Egypt. Russian Jews at that time played an important part in the Revolution, and the Minister of Justice in the new regime was a Jew, and an Orthodox Jew to boot, Yitzchak Steinberg. Now that the Jewish problem of Russia was solved, the Zionist solution seemed to be superfluous. After all, the most pressing problem had been that of Russian Jewry. This was at least the opinion of many leading Jews. Weizmann thought otherwise. "The sufferings of the Russian Jews," he said in a speech in London in 1917, "were never the cause of Zionism. The fundamental cause of Zionism was, and is, the ineradicable national striving of Jewry to have a house of its own — a national center, a national home with a national Jewish life. And this remains now stronger than ever. A strong and free Russian Jewry will appreciate more than ever the strivings of the Zionist Organization." Little did he and others know how soon this "strong and free Russian Jewry" would have to succumb to the severe restrictions of the Bolshevik regime.

The Balfour Declaration spoke carefully about the obligation to safeguard the rights of the population of Palestine, meaning the Arabs without ever mentioning them by name. But it was clearly understood by everyone that an amicable agreement with the Arabs had to be sought. The agreements which England had made with the Arabs are too well known to be recorded here. There was important Arabophile sentiment in Great Britain, and Lawrence of Arabia, who lived among the Arabs, was much more than a British agent. His *Seven Pillars of Wisdom* is eloquent testimony to a very deep and genuine friendship for the Arabs. It was important for the Zionists to win Arab support, or at least gain their understanding of the aims of the Zionist movement and allay their fears. Weizmann undertook this task. His visit to Emir Faisal in 1918, while the war was still raging, is one of the most exciting episodes in Zionist history. Weizmann himself was a man of great historic perception. Very often he would pause to muse about the strange course of Jewish history and the role which he was destined to play in it. He undertook the journey with the help and knowledge of the British, together with Major Ormsby-Gore (later Lord Harlech). Emir Faisal, son of Husein, Sherif of Mecca and later King of Syria, received Weizmann in Aqaba. Weizmann reminisced about this visit in his memoirs:

> It was a brilliant moonlit night — Palestinian moonlight — and I looked down from Moab on the Jordan Valley and the Dead Sea and the Judean hills beyond. I may have been a little lightheaded from the sudden change of climate, but as I stood there I suddenly had the feeling that three thousand years had vanished, had become as nothing. Here I was, on the identical ground, on the identical errand, of my ancestors in the dawn of my people's history, when they came to negotiate with the ruler of the country for a right of way, that they may return to their home.

The meeting with Faisal in the presence of T. E. Lawrence, whose views were more favorable to Zionist aims than those of his countrymen in the military administration of Palestine, proved a great success. At times, the services of an interpreter could be dispensed with when Faisal changed from Arabic to French. It made the two-hour-long conversation easier. There were mutual trust and agreement. "We are working together," Faisal said, "for a reformed and revived Near East, and our two movements complete one another. The Jewish movement is national and not imperialist. Our movement is national and not imperialist, and there is room in Syria for us both. Indeed, I think that neither can be a real success without the other." The views were later confirmed in a letter addressed to Justice Felix Frankfurter, then still a professor of law and a member of the "Zionist Commission." Not very much later the views of the Arabs changed. Today the meeting with Faisal is a painful reminder of the fact that such a meeting would be impossible. The Arabs never conceived of Jewish suffering in terms of their own Islamic responsibility, but charged this responsibility to the Christian world. Never once, either at the time of Faisal or now, did they consider the degradation to which Jews living in Moslem countries are subjected. Until this very day they have refused to concern themselves with Jewish fate, and even Jews with the number of Auschwitz tattooed on their arms are to them "imperialist agents" living for no good reason and with no justification upon Arab soil.

The Balfour Declaration preceded by a month the successful conclusion of the military campaign in Palestine against the Turkish forces under German command. Lord Allenby's conquest of Jerusalem culminated the operations which had begun in the region of the Suez Canal and which pursued the Turkish army via Beersheba and Gaza to Jerusalem. The Zionists always insisted that Jewish brigades be permitted to fight along with the Allies. There were many good reasons for pressing this demand. One was obviously prompted by national pride. The Jewish people were no longer a ghetto people. If Palestine was to be their national home, they wanted to participate in the battle of liberation, and Jewish blood should mingle with that of others. The time when Jews were begging for charity was gone. A people which deserves the name of a nation might fight for its homeland. This was from the very beginning part of the Zionist ideology. It played a very important part in the period between the Balfour Declaration and the proclamation of independence in 1948. Even in the earliest time of Jewish settlements, defense groups had been formed, *shomrim,* which protected Jewish fields and vineyards against marauders and fought later in the Arab-Jewish skirmishes. The Jewish Legion, formed by American and Canadian Jews in 1917, and Joseph Trumpeldor's Zion Mule Corps were the forerunners of the Jewish Army. The "Jewish Brigade" which fought along with British units not only distinguished itself during the Second World War, but made the first Jewish contacts with the Jews liberated from Hitler's death camps. The active participation of Jewish military units in the two wars served as training ground for the army of the coming state. This does not minimize the moral motivation of the Jewish participation in the First and Second World Wars. But it does not eliminate the practical consequences either.

The years between 1917 and 1948 constituted the most difficult period in the preparation for statehood. From the very beginning the Balfour Declaration was bound to create both potentials and difficulties. It seemed to try too hard to avoid all possible difficulties. Some of these formulations were arrived at with tongue in cheek. The Arab problem was not spelled out. It seemed as though there was hardly a problem outside of the safeguarding of "non-Jewish rights." In fact, there had been clear obligations solemnly undertaken by the British. Arab independence was part of the British strategy for victory in the Near East. To speak of the Jewish national home *in* Palestine instead of a clear avowal of Palestine *as* the Jewish national home of the future was to invite difficulties in the future. In the atmosphere of the Faisal undertakings, it might have been possible to avoid animosity, hatred and bloodshed. Whatever was left vague had to be defined later. The mandate was given to Britain by the League of Nations, and even this act was preceded by many negotiations which were to reach agreement of the terms under which Britain was to administer the country. When the Zionists pressed for a recognition of their "historic claim" to Palestine (the only plausible basis for legal immigration and final possession of the country), the term which was accepted was "historical connection." It sounded like a clever evasion of the issue. And it was an evasion; when realities began to press, Churchill, then the Secretary of Colonies, had to emphasize that the Jews were in Palestine "as of right and not as of sufferance." Everybody proceeded in accordance with what he considered to be his right. The Jews had the Balfour Declaration and the assurances of the League of Nations. The Arabs had similar assurances. It was a clash of right with right. However, while the Arabs watched the reawakening of Arab lands and nations which had succumbed to negligence and corruption under the Ottoman Empire, the Jews witnessed the destruction of their most prosperous communities. While vast areas of land blessed with the richest oil possessions of the world supported only small numbers of people and cried out for new developments and immigration, the Jewish world crumbled before the very eyes of humanity. To the

Jews the Balfour Declaration was not merely a piece of paper with international guarantees inscribed upon it; it was a matter of life and death.

While 1918 brought revolutions and self-determination to many countries of the world, and with it promises of emancipation and freedom for the Jews, these promises proved a mirage. Germany was a classic example. In 1918 the Kaiser was forced to abdicate, and a new democratic Germany came into being for the first time in its history. With it Jews began to play an important role in political leadership. No longer was this leadership limited to liberal parties. Jews became members of the cabinet. For the first time in Germany's history, a Jew was appointed Secretary of Foreign Affairs. Walter Rathenau, an outstanding engineer who was instrumental in the development of Germany's General Electric Company (formerly headed by his father), a cultured, democratic German Jew whose ambivalent and often negative attitude toward his Jewish origin is a classic example of Jewish psychopathology, was assassinated by two high school boys. He had served Germany as Minister of Reconstruction and had been its Foreign Minister for less than a year. The two boys were members of a racist, anti-Semitic group which could not endure the thought of a Jew representing Germany's government. The summer of 1922, when this murder was committed, will remain unforgettable to those of us who were students at the University of Berlin at that time. Only the blind could not see the hatred that lived in the hearts of our fellow students at that time. It seemed too difficult for them and many of the professors of the famous, ancient university to conceal their satisfaction. This does not mean that there were not voices of serious politicians and men of public life who warned against the danger that emanated from the German reactionaries. Everybody could clearly see that the assassination had been inspired by growing anti-Semitism and antiliberalism. It was not merely the Jews who were in danger. It was democracy itself that was hated. It took another eleven years for Hitler to seize power in Germany, but even in 1922 there were German universities which made it impossible for Jewish students to pursue their academic training there. The famous University of Jena, for instance, had adopted a clear anti-Semitic policy and was not ashamed to proclaim it publicly. While the Jews seemed satisfied that the Messianic times had finally come, the signs which predicted disaster for them were unmistakable. The beginning of the great tragedy of inflation, which ruined the lives and wiped out the savings of millions of the middle class and particularly the recipients of monthly pensions (a very numerous group in Central Europe), created the proper conditions for demagogues and their propaganda.

The situation was much worse in Poland. Three and

a half million Jews were living there in the hope that Poland would live up to the solemn undertaking concluded on June 28, 1919, which guaranteed equal treatment to citizens. The provisions of this treaty, guaranteeing minority rights to Jews, became part of Poland's democratic constitution in 1922. Although the Pilsudski regime, which came to power in 1926, rejected anti-Semitism as an official policy, it was in no position to combat the growing popular anti-Semitism, an ancient Polish tradition, now encouraged by rampant anti-Semitism in neighboring Germany. After Pilsudski's death, the government was no longer so timid. It adopted anti-Semitism as its official policy, and the Parliament became an effective forum for anti-Semitic propaganda. Polish Jewry's economic situation, never particularly good, had worsened after the First World War. A government-sponsored campaign against Jewish shopkeepers forced thousands out of business. Blessed by the church and legalized by the government, this systematic picketing and boycott of Jewish business enterprises rendered Polish Jewry nearly bankrupt. Soon 40 per cent of the entire Jewish population of Poland had to be considered destitute and was in need of charity provided by American Jewry.

In the meantime the interpretation of the Balfour Declaration and the implementation of the mandate assumed tragic proportions. The Jews were eager to develop Palestine toward the day when the promise of self-government would be fulfilled. While the political struggle dominated the headlines, a quiet process of colonization and preparation for statehood went on. Land was bought from Arab absentee landlords who proclaimed publicly that they were ardent, nationalistic Arab patriots but who privately and often clandestinely sold their land to the Jewish National Fund, the official administrator of Jewish land. The Jewish settlements were established in accordance with a careful plan which placed *kibbutzim* in strategic areas in terms of both military defense and the determination of boundaries for the state. These single-minded men, most of them members of agricultural settlements who lived and worked with the vision of the coming state in their hearts, played a vital role for the future. The northern area of Israel, Galilee, would be Arab territory today had it not been for these unsung heroes of agricultural preparation. But of course the main struggle was political. It was clear that the future of a Jewish Palestine could no longer be considered a Zionist project. All of Jewry was to be involved in an enterprise which was now more than a political-historical dream. Palestine, as everybody conceded, had to play a vital role in the practical solution of the Jewish problem. The formation of the Jewish Agency, the first non-Zionist body, acted as a temporary foreign office of the quasi-government of the state-to-be. Louis Marshall, Felix Warburg, Léon Blum and Oscar Wassermann, none of them Zionists, lent the prestige of their status in America, France and Germany to the upbuilding of Palestine. Leading Jews of other countries joined this new group. The political direction remained in the hands of Weizmann and the Jewish party leaders in Palestine. Negotiations with England and other governments were now more important than ever. The era of interpretation and implementation needed patience in the face of nationalistic passion and quiet determination in the face of much yielding and compromise.

The situation which developed was a tragedy of hatred, misunderstanding, ill will and outright brutality. The Jews took the provisions of the mandate seriously. They were in Palestine to build a Jewish State. The British government assured them of their rights but counseled restraint. The British military and civil administration, used to dealing with docile "natives," found Jewish determination and alertness obnoxious and disturbing. Never before had they dealt with such obstinate, strong-willed and opinionated people. Some Englishmen, imbued with the old English love for the Bible, admired the Old Testamentarian fervor of the Jews. The most outstanding of such men was Orde Wingate, that extraordinary, imaginative, stubborn Englishman who trained Jewish lads in the art of guerrilla warfare, and who became the real founder of the Haganah, the Jewish Army. Others were unashamedly anti-Semitic. The Arabs, deserted by their landed gentry, who preferred to live in Paris while exploiting Palestinians, and led by ambitious and ferocious nationalists such as the Grand Mufti of Jerusalem, resorted to a policy of pogroms and protests. Several bloody outbursts took place between 1920 and 1938. The local administration was unwilling to cope with these pogroms since they sympathized with them. The government in London, which had now decided that the Balfour Declaration was a major blunder and that British policy in the Near East had to be based on Arab friendship, began a policy of restricted immigration. Several royal commissions were sent to Palestine and made their recommendations, most of which suggested further restrictions. The famous Peel Commission in 1937 suggested for the first time partition as the only solution. In 1939 a White Paper decreed a total immigration of seventy-five thousand Jews, after which the mandate should be considered fully implemented. For the Jews (and, one might think, also for the world) events had made such a decision unacceptable. Hitler had become the leader of Germany in 1933, and the problem of immigration had become a question of life and death. In 1938, a year before the White Paper was published, all German synagogues had gone up in flames. Jews were deported by the hundreds of thousands, and the destinations of the deportation trains were places like Auschwitz and Bergen-Belsen. Himmler reigned supreme, and a man by the name of Adolf Eichmann was in charge of Hitler's policy, the total extermination of the Jews. Since other countries, including the United States, had established immigration quotas rigidly enforced by many an American consul in Europe, the desperation of the Jewish people seemed a reasonable attitude.

The fact that Hitler had chosen the Jews (altogether there were only five hundred and fifty thousand in all of Germany, less than 1 per cent of the total population) as his main target created a clever smoke screen for world opinion. The world had become accustomed to anti-Jewish persecution. The years between the two world wars witnessed the heyday of anti-Semitism in the United States. Nobody really cared about the Jews. When on April 1, 1933, Hitler declared an official boycott against the Jews, the world was not deeply moved. To those like myself, who were there to witness the strange spectacle of young, arrogant brown-uniformed storm troopers standing in front of Jewish shops and department stores, preventing "Aryans" from entering, this day will be remembered as a prelude to genocide. The Jews, those patriotic, trusting, optimistic German Jews whose fatherland had thus betrayed them, were too stunned to comprehend the seriousness of the situation. To some it seemed like an exercise of youthful exuberance, a sort of political mischief day which would soon be followed by more orderly, reserved and conciliatory government measures. Only a few took Hitler so seriously that they believed his threats would ever be carried out. After all, there were the large number of good, decent Germans. Soon they would stop him in his tracks, and after the young Nazis had had their day, the old Prussian discipline and order would prevail. It was no more than an episode. It could not possibly be more. Hindenburg was still in office. This was sufficient guarantee for a return to sobriety and reason. This, at least, was the thinking of many of the Jewish leaders who had preached assimilation all along and were opposed to Zionism and Palestine, cautioning the people against rash actions such as hasty emigration.

The people themselves were deeply frightened. The first of April was a Saturday. I was then a rabbi of the Jewish community in Berlin, the youngest among many elderly, highly respected colleagues. The services held in my synagogue on the Friday night, the eve of the boycott, will never be forgotten. Every seat in the large synagogue was taken. People stood in the aisles. An atmosphere of frightened solemnity hovered over all of them. Never in my life had I seen people so deeply moved and visibly numbed by a fate they felt was descending upon them like a tornado, threatening to demolish everything in its path. There stood and sat thousands of people, many of whom had never before attended a synagogue service, converted Jews, peripheral Jews, atheists, cynics, together with the small group of the pious and fervent. Never in all my life will I forget the moment when the congregation was to rise to proclaim the oneness of God in the ancient: "Hear, O Israel, the Lord Our God is One." The organ was silenced and the choir inaudible, for there suddenly rose from the breasts, the innermost parts of these Jewish men and women, an outcry so savage, a mixture of despair and hope, of faith and a sense of return and identification, that the melody was lost and all that was left was the bitter cry of a people suddenly united in common misery. Such scenes had been unknown since the Middle Ages. In the orderly, well-regimented atmosphere of a liberal temple, where any kind of spontaneity would have been considered foreign and exotic, this was a strange and stirring sight. In all of the Hitler regime, this was to me the most memorable experience. It was not merely an exhibition of despair. It was a great demonstration of solidarity, of the sudden comprehension of Jewish fate and destiny. It was, to the German Jews, the great moment of the discovery of their deep Jewish roots. It was a moment of return.

The records of suffering and mass murder have all but obliterated the story of Jewish creativity which

German Jews stimulated during these first few years of the Hitler regime until the days of deportation when it was no longer possible. More Jewish books were published during these first five years, from 1933 to 1938, than were burned in the famous act of book burning. Under the threat of death and danger, a movement of return to Jewish values and a return also to Jewish peoplehood took place which at times looked like a Jewish renaissance. A Jewry dwindling in numbers, decreasing more and more as the years went by, suddenly clung to the heritage as the only source of comfort. The Jewish people were eager to learn their history, which might yield some clue to their suffering. They began to read the classics of Zionism and to understand Jewish fate. They began to sing the songs of the Jewish people, and they flocked to the synagogues, where with their fellow Jews they felt safe, at least for as long as the service lasted.

Everything outside had been turned into a strange ghetto, a ghetto without walls. They continued to live among their Christian neighbors, but the neighbors no longer saw them. It was a life without neighbors. Old friends no longer greeted them. The Christian servants had to leave their homes. The Jewish children had to be transferred from their public schools to purely Jewish schools. Theaters were no longer open to them. Concert halls were closed to them. The invisible walls were everywhere. The meadows, the mountains, the woods of Germany no longer welcomed Jews, and even the benches in the public parks bore signs which forbade them to sit down. Soon the stores were open for Jews only in the late hours of the day when most of the food was gone; the streetcars and buses no longer took as passengers those who had to wear on their clothes a yellow star with the word JUDE printed across it in German letters imitating Hebrew characters. Life had become not merely dangerous but empty. Physicians and lawyers were no longer able to practice. The musicians who were discovered to have had a Jewish grandmother, let alone those of Jewish blood, could no longer play the cello or the piano in public; the artists no longer exhibited, and the architects were out of work. Children could not play in public playgrounds; their Christian playmates refused to play with them, and many threw stones at them when they saw them. The Jews of Germany, who had lived there for sixteen hundred years, were outcasts in the land of their great-grandparents' birth. I speak not of blood and murder. The assassination of the souls, the humiliation and degradation of the human beings preceded the mass murder in the camps.

Degradation played an important part in the scheme of arousing the kind of mass hatred which would ultimately lead to mass murder. It was not at all easy to create the proper psychological conditions for this undertaking. The Jews had to be dehumanized before even Nazis were ready to exterminate them. The very term "extermination" applies to vermin, not to people. The Jews had to be insulted, humbled, degraded and humiliated, deprived of human dignity and pronounced inferior. (The most revealing experience which I had with the Gestapo in Berlin was not brutality, but an interrogation at its headquarters at the very beginning of the Hitler regime, in 1933. I was asked to make a statement on an alleged accusation against me. The Gestapo agent listened to my statement and then he said: "I would like to believe you. Unfortunately, you are not capable of telling the truth. You are a Jew. You are a liar by birth." He was a rather friendly man, and the very fact that there was no harshness, no threat in the tone of his voice was most frightening. He was not a monster. He was a Nazi. He was a Superman. I was a Jew. According to Nazi ideology I was an *Untermensch*, less than a human.)

This process of dehumanization took a long time. In spite of all the anti-Semitic propaganda, it took the Nazis five years before mass deportations were undertaken. Hitler came to power in 1933. The burning of the synagogues, the signal for deportations and the "final solution" took place in 1938. Eichmann's career begins in the same year. Even after the arrival of the death trains in the concentration camps, only the deformed, the pregnant and the sick were sent to the gas chambers. The healthy ones were sent to labor camps to work and to starve until they became so emaciated and skeletonized that they no longer resembled human beings. Only then were the Nazis ready to send them to their death. Some of the tormentors might have assuaged their consciences by assuring themselves that their victims were no longer eager to live and that it was merciful to kill them. On the strange "planets" called Auschwitz, Bergen-Belsen and Dachau, victims and persecutors lived and died in accordance with new rules, never before known to man.

The story of mass murder and every conceivable form of brutality has been told during the Eichmann trial. I need not repeat it here. Nobody will ever be able to really understand the degree of bestiality to which so many Germans had succumbed. The mass graves of Bergen-Belsen and Auschwitz, which contain the bodies of hundreds of thousands of victims, and the gas chambers and the crematoria are the silent witnesses of all the outrages committed there. It is an insult to the Middle Ages to call them medieval. It is impossible to think of a normal, unburdened relationship of the Jewish people with Germans, however great and sincere the efforts of the German government and others may be. It will take many generations of Germans and Jews to forget these years of horror. When Hitler was finally defeated at the cost of death to millions of young men of every creed and nationality, Europe was a heap of rubble such as the world had never seen. When American, British, French and Russian soldiers opened the heavy gates of the concentration camps, they found thousands of unburied bodies scattered all over the area and an equal number of emaciated, skeletonized human beings too weak to move and greet the liberators. There were thousands of Christians among the dead and the living. In the tale of Jewish misery they are sometimes forgotten. But the Jewish people had suffered most grievously. The number of the six million has become a symbol of horror rather than a statistical figure. The attempt made by some Germans to prove to the world that "only" five million died is an obscene exercise of statisticians which parallels the crimes which were committed. There is obviously no punishment that could be considered just, and no restitution will ever be possible to eradicate the guilt that must lie heavily upon the conscience of the German people and upon all of Christendom. That the civilized world should have been so lethargic in the face of this great human tragedy called for a collective act of atonement. The creation of the State of Israel constitutes just that. The meeting of the General Assembly on that fateful Saturday afternoon of November 29 in the year 1947 was the great Yom Kippur of mankind. Those of us who attended the meeting were overcome with the solemnity of the proceedings. This was not merely a political act. The affirmative vote of each delegation which made possible the creation of a national home for the homeless was an affirmation of faith. It was a religious act of penitence. There was no other way to pay a debt to the six million than to create a country in which the survivors of the great earthquake could live in new dignity.

The situation in Palestine had become untenable. The Jews, unable to witness the torture of their people, organized that "illegal" immigration which has become the great saga of action born of desperation. The little ships, many of them so rickety that only desperate men and women would entrust their lives to them, landed during the hours of the night at the deserted beaches of Palestine — still under British mandate, which barred immigration. A new desperate courage had swept the country. Small bands of armed men and women made the perilous journey from Europe across the ocean, most of them untrained in the art of seafaring. Many Christians in lands which had to be traversed understood the meaning of these long tracks of people, and helped. The Italian people played a particularly heroic part in it. The Christian people of Denmark, under the leadership of the royal family, had set an example of Christian heroism when they shipped all their Jews on little crafts to safety. Many of the illegal ships did not arrive. Some were scuttled, some were intercepted; and Jews, fathers, mothers and little children, veterans of concentration camps, were taken to similar camps under British rule. The armed bands of Jewish militiamen in Palestine, trained in guerrilla warfare, received those who arrived, and soon they were scattered all over the country. The British government, under the unyielding guidance of Ernest Bevin, the Foreign Minister, faced with open revolt, massacre, bombings, sabotage, and above all, the determination of a desperate people, understood that the era of the mandate had ended. No orderly administration was possible when all the arguments of decency and reason weighed so heavily in favor of a Jewish independent state. The International Commission of the United Nations had recommended the partition of Palestine with so much earnestness and urgency that Britain could not dare defy the world community. There were enough important men in England itself who counseled withdrawal from Palestine. Sir Winston Churchill was one of them.

However solemn and magnanimous the decision of November 29 was, the United Nations could do nothing to enforce its own decision. It became clear that the implementation of partition could not be carried out without the use of armed forces. The United States, which had voted for the decision, began to change its attitude. The State Department was never too happy about the affirmative vote. America now suggested that the country be placed under the trusteeship of the United Nations. While uncertainty and fears gripped the United Nations and the Jews, and while the discussions were still in full swing, the Jews of Palestine decided to take matters into their own hands. On the fourteenth of May, 1948, David Ben-Gurion proclaimed the creation of the new state. It was to bear the proud, historic, ancient name: Israel. In spite of reluctance and even hostility in the State Department, Harry Truman, the President of the United States, announced recognition of the Jewish State. Three days later the Soviet Union announced its *de jure* recognition. The rest is history: the Arab-Jewish war, the victory which proved the military prowess and the sacrificial spirit of Israel, her admission to the United Nations and the establishment of a new fact in the history of the world and in the life of the Jewish people. Not since the days when the exiles of Babylonia were led back to the homeland had such great and overwhelming revolution occurred in Jewish life. The psalm which was sung by the returnees in the sixth century B.C. leaped to life again. On the lips of the twentieth-century Jews it had an ancient ring but a new meaning:

> *When the Lord brought back those that returned to Zion,*
> *We were like unto them that dream.*

Then was our mouth filled with laughter,
And our tongue with singing;
Then said they among the nations:
"The Lord hath done great things with these."
"The Lord hath done great things with us.
We rejoice."
Turn our captivity, O Lord,
As the streams in the Negev.
They that sow in tears
Shall reap in joy.

Zionism was the greatest and most creative force in modern Jewry. Now that the goal of the movement, the "creation of an internationally guaranteed Jewish national home in Palestine," has been fulfilled, Zionism finds itself in the position of a movement which has to redefine its functions. At a time when all possible Jewish functions, religious, social, educational and others, have been preempted by organizations with a long record of achievement in these fields, a mere redefinition of functions will prove unsuccessful. It is not easy for a movement which once had such unparalleled and vital functions in Jewish life to simply disappear and declare its purpose achieved. But the fact remains that it has no particular function in contemporary Jewish life which is not now fulfilled by other groups or that could not be better performed by combined efforts. It is more than obvious that Zionism as a political movement aiming to establish a Jewish State in Israel simply has no function.

To many Jews Zionism was a religion. It is not easy for them to accept the fact that the Messiah has come. Fulfillment is always an anticlimax. Nothing is more marvelous than a dream. Nothing is more disappointing than reality. The more Utopian the dream, the more frustrating is the reality. Theodor Herzl's grandiose prophecy of the new generations of Maccabees that would rise in the new land can now be tested. It is true that Israel has many heroes, but the Israelis will not permit a romanticization of land or people. Leon Uris's *Exodus* was violently rejected in Israel because it depicted a nation of romantic, dedicated heroes. They are in reality what every people should be, a nation of normal people.

The State of Israel has come into being, and this fact poses new questions and creates new dilemmas and even calamities. While it was the dream of freedom and independence of the Jews organized in the Zionist movement, it was a great and noble goal. Now Israel is a sovereign state. The younger and smaller a state, the more jealously does it watch its sovereignty. Israel is very jealous of its sovereignty. It knows that it cannot speak for the Jews outside of Israel, and whenever it does so not only does it trespass into the precincts of the Jewish communities, but it also forfeits its own sovereignty. Sovereignty is the right of a state over its own territory and the people who live within the boundaries of this territory. Not more and not less. Zionism, as I have tried to show, was the Jewish people "on its way home." It created with great ingenuity institutions of the movement which could easily become institutions of the state if and when it was proclaimed. This and the scope and wisdom of the concrete preparations for the state are the historic value of the Zionist movement. Everything became the training ground for the state-to-be. For decades the sons of peddlers and small shopkeepers learned the art of diplomacy, political negotiations, agricultural planning, governmental finances and even warfare. It was this long apprenticeship which made the state possible. Today the apprentices have taken over. They have become prime ministers, secretaries of foreign affairs, finance, agriculture and education. The Zionist "parties" which represented certain ideologies in the Zionist movement are now political parties of a sovereign state. The Zionist Congress is now the Knesset, the Parliament of Israel. While until 1948 the Zionists acted as if there *were* a state, they now act as if there were *no* state. In terms of the desperate attempt of a movement to preserve itself, this can be understood. In terms of the interests of a new Jewish future, it cannot be permitted to exist. The Jews, including those who support the Zionist movement, must at long last recognize, *de jure* and *de facto,* the existence of the sovereign State of Israel.

"The Zionist movement as a whole," writes David Ben-Gurion, the Prime Minister of Israel, "has lost its meaning because its aspirations have been realized. The establishment of the State made all Jews 'friends of Israel' and an American Zionist is no more a 'friend' of Israel than any other Jew." This is probably a simplification. It disregards those of the younger generation who have yet to find a relationship to Israel. But there can be little disagreement about his main premise, that Zionism as Herzl knew it and as Zionists knew it makes little sense today. It is not merely that the Zionist dream is fulfilled. This is only part of the story. The whole Zionist ideology, which presupposes a deterioration of Jewish positions all over the Diaspora, is no longer valid. The whole ideological apparatus, so valid and so potent in the nineteenth century and even until Hitler came to power, has lost its value in today's world. The dream is fulfilled and there is no longer any fear of impending nightmares. This new Jewish generation in the free world lives beyond nightmare and dream. It lives under a new freedom with new problems and challenges, to be sure. But the questions are new and so are the answers.

To the Jews Israel is first and foremost a Jewish State. It was created for the purpose of solving the problem of Jewish homelessness. No Jew can afford to remain aloof from an undertaking that is based upon such high moral purposes and one that has saved the lives of so many hundreds of thousands of fellow Jews. It would be a sign of ingratitude, to say the least, if now that Israel has solved the major Jewish problem the Jews should simply withdraw and leave the young and brave country to its own devices. Israel continues to receive Jews from all over the world. It is, no doubt, the safest and best place for Jews who want to live as Jews.

Israel's purpose, however, is not merely to serve as a haven of refuge. The Israeli "Law of the Ingathering" is one of the great documents in our history. It is the free, proud, moral declaration of brotherhood issued by a people which had been dragged through the furnaces of persecution. But this is not the only purpose of Israel, nor is sovereignty and statehood an end of its own. One of the great purposes of Jewish statehood is the creation of conditions under which Jews can continue to make their own Hebraic contribution to world civilization. For the first time in two thousand years the Jews are a majority in their own land, speaking their own language, building their own cities, bridges and roads, tilling their own fields, fighting their own wars. For the first time there are new generations of Jewish farmers, far removed from the neuroses of the city, from competition and the bitter struggle for physical survival. A people which has given such good account of itself can be expected to create extraordinary things in a land of its own. The Jews believe that their last word has not yet been spoken and that much needs to be said or sung or painted or sculptured or written, and that they may be able to do just this. Israel is that opportunity. It is therefore the greatest challenge not merely to Jewish *ingenuity* but to the genius of Israel.

I am afraid that in the first decade of its existence it was the admiration for ingenuity that won out. It is only natural that the Jews and Israelis should admire the new uniforms, the aircraft, the ministerial titles, the flags, the stamps and all the other trappings of statehood. Jews are very proud to have ministers and diplomats of their own, and in this justifiable but childish pride they often overestimate the trappings of the state. They sometimes behave like a poor family when one of its own has "made good." But this attitude will, I feel sure, disappear and give way to an appreciation of the more important functions of Israel. In Israel itself there is much provincial chauvinism which creates wrong perspectives and false hopes. It is not merely sobriety that is needed in Israel and the Jewish communities of the world. What is needed is a more profound understanding of the real purposes of the country. Without such understanding Israel is in danger of becoming a machine, albeit a very efficient one, and its people glorified Levantines. Since much of the immigration comes from Levantine countries where scratching the surface is the extent of thinking and living, the danger is very real. Israeli leaders are very much aware of it. A young state needs constant reappraisal, and the checks and balances must not be merely political but also moral and, in the deepest sense, religious. The Jewish State has, at times, obligations which force it to disregard expediency and choose the more difficult and even detrimental moral solution.

There is therefore hope that world Jewry will benefit from Israel's creativity. The record of the last decade or so justifies these hopes, at least in the field of scholastic endeavors, both in the area of general sciences and the narrower sphere of Judaistic studies. The revival of the Hebrew language alone is of tremendous importance to the inner life of the Jew. The area in which Israel fails us most tragically is religion, the chief concern of the Jewish people. Nothing has come from Jerusalem, not even a word. Against all expectations of a great renaissance of Judaism, what has emerged so far is the most debased form of religion: ritualism and politics. Neither compassion, forthright moral leadership, nor any attempt to find religious answers to the many perplexing questions of the world and the country itself has been forthcoming. Whether this hope for the prophet's "word of the Lord from Jerusalem" will ever be realized in our own time is very doubtful, and world Jewry will have to find its own answers to the future of Judaism as an organized religion.

But it is too early, and it is probably also unfair, to present a catalogue of benefits that accrue to the Jewish communities because Israel exists. It is naïve and even preposterous to think of Israel in such terms. It was not created for the purpose of solving the problems of the Jews outside of Israel, and Israel's *raison d'être* cannot and must not be measured by an assessment of its direct contributions to these communities. The great Jewish thinker Achad Haam conceived of the Jewish State as a sun sending its warm rays into world Jewry. To him the only real purpose of a homeland was to provide new life for the Jews in the Diaspora. But this cannot be expected to happen within the first few years. It may never happen. Israel may develop within its own context and needs. When the old generation of European Jews will have died and the sabras seize the reins of Israel, many things may happen which might render mutual influences impossible. In the meantime, however, Jews must acknowledge their indebtedness to Israel in terms best expressed by Karl Shapiro in a poem* written for the celebration of the founding of the state:

* Karl Shapiro, *Poems of a Jew*, p. 4.

When I think of the liberation of Palestine,
When my eye conceives the great black English
> *line*
Spanning the world news of two thousand years,
My heart leaps forward like a hungry dog,
My heart is thrown back on its tangled chain,
My soul is hangdog in a Western chair.

When I think of the battle for Zion I hear
The drop of chains, the starting forth of feet,
And I remain chained in a Western chair.
My blood beats like a bird against the wall,
I feel the weight of prisons in my skull
Falling away; my forbears stare through stone.

When I see the name of Israel high in print
The fences crumble in my flesh; I sink
Deep in my Western chair and rest my soul.
I look the stranger clear to the blue depths
Of his unclouded eye. I say my name
Aloud for the first time unconsciously.

Speak of the tillage of a million heads
No more. Speak of the evil myth no more
Of one who harried Jesus on his way
Saying, Go faster. Speak no more
Of the yellow badge, decta nefaria.
Speak the name only of the living land.

It is in such poetic terms that we must think of Israel's great mission in the life of contemporary Jewry. It has, by its sheer existence, wiped out the

burden which lay on a whole people, being pronounced guilty and sentenced to die for crimes which
they did not commit. It has suddenly turned our eyes
from the countless cemeteries and gas chambers toward the green fields and the mountains "whence my
hope cometh." It has removed the stench of death
from our nostrils and let us, for the first time in two
thousand years, breathe in the fresh air of an early
spring morning. It has remade the image of the Jew,
the eternal sufferer, hoary and emaciated, into that of
a young, strong man "laughing at the time to come,"
and preparing for a long and marvelous life. It has
placed a brand-new cradle in Jewish life and written
"Birth" all over it. Birth, and not death. Life, and not
decay. It has raised the stature of every Jew in the
world. It has straightened our backs. It has brightened
our eyes. For this, for this alone, the Jews of the world
must bless the fourteenth day of May in the year nine-
teen hundred and forty-eight. This day not only has
given birth to a new state, but has given a new lease
on life to the Jewish people all over the world.

The Dilemma

of the Modern

Jew

ANOTHER NEW REALITY BESIDES THE STATE of Israel has now emerged: the phenomenon called American Jewry. It has no parallel in Jewish history. Each century creates its own phenomena, its own problems and promises. So must American Jewry be judged and understood within its own setting, as part of the American society itself, a new (and often misunderstood) factor in the history of man. It is important not merely because it constitutes the largest Jewish community that ever existed anywhere in the world during the thousands of years of Jewish history. (There are probably more than five and a half million Jews in the United States, although there are no reliable statistics.) American Jewry's importance lies in its social structure, its great potential and its unique problems. They require special attention.

To begin with, American Jewry is not merely the largest but also the youngest Jewish community. While it is true that the first Jews reached the port of New Amsterdam in 1654 and that there have been Jews in the United States ever since, it is equally true that the majority of American Jews began to arrive at the end of the nineteenth century. During the American Revolution, only two thousand Jews lived in the colonies, and the seven thousand Jews who fought in the armies engaged in the Civil War (six thousand in the Union army and one thousand with the Confederates) represented a total Jewish population of but one hundred and fifty thousand. But from 1881 to 1914, more than two million Jews left pogrom-ridden czarist Russia to find homes in the United States. This community of immigrants has now grown to its numerical strength of more than five million.

American Jewry is no longer a group of immigrants. More than 75 per cent are native Americans. The American-Jewish "problem" is with the second and third generations. Both their occupational structure (which has changed considerably since the days when Jewish immigrant tailors worked in sweatshops for less than fifteen dollars a week) and their family ties lured them into the large cities, so that today 40 per cent live in New York City. The bulk of the Jewish population (75 per cent) is distributed over only fourteen large communities. The general move to the suburbs, in which the Jews participate together with other middle-class groups in the country, has created some new phenomena, problems as well as hopes.

American Jewry, which began its history with the immigration of Sephardic Jews from Brazil and other Spanish-Portuguese backgrounds and was expanded by the period of German Jewish immigration during and after the 1840s, is now for all practical purposes (and with far-reaching consequences) a community of East European origin. The leadership which was in the hands of Jews of German descent (the Lehmans, the Schiffs and the Warburgs in the field of philanthropy; and people like Justice Brandeis, Ludwig Lewisohn, Louis Untermeyer, Guggenheim and the Straus family in their own fields) has now passed into the hands of Jews of East European origin. The distinction between the groups is no longer of any importance today. There might still be some social snobbishness among the old-timers, but the younger generation simply disregards these and other group distinctions. The young Jews of East European descent "intermarry" with no compunction into German Jewish families, and vice versa. The prevalence of East European Jews has played an important role in the emotional makeup of the American Jew. It has brought a new intensity in Jewish life, an indefinable quality without which American Jewry would not be what it is today. Since very few of those who create the general mood in American Jewry were born in the ghettos of Russia and Poland, it is difficult to find a rational explanation for the deep and abiding sense of identification, not merely with Jewish misery in the world and participation in the building of the State of Israel, but with "Jewishness" altogether. It is quite true that the Lower East Side of New York and its counterparts in other cities, where many of today's father generations spent their youth, was a ghetto too. But the same spirit seems to permeate many of the younger set who could have received such impulses only through osmosis or that nebulous, irrational process called "collective memory." At any rate, it is there, at least for the time being, and it is there as a factor underlying many of the more rational Jewish enterprises of the community. This is an unusual phenomenon for Jews who are deeply integrated into America and its general concerns. It is quite different from similarly "assimilated" (the term has to be closely examined) communities as in Western Europe.

When the emotional factors, which seem to be at the bottom of all the motivations which propel a great many Jewish activities — religious, philanthropical and organizational — are scrutinized, they might turn out to be a conglomerate of many things: outside pressures, strong family tradition, a need for identification, a sense of belonging, national pride, a sentimental and indefinable attachment to memories, compliance with the general structure of the community (particularly in the suburbs and small towns which call for church affiliation), and probably a great many other factors. This affirmation of belongingness is as yet not expressed in strong religious convictions. The question of the deeper meaning of being a Jew has still been left open. Yet the quest for it has begun. A large number of books dealing with the "essence" of Judaism attest to this urge. But the question which has plagued Israel during the heated debate of "Who is a Jew?" is irrelevant for American Jewry. It is a matter of *existence* and fact rather than the result of a theological debate. No definition is felt necessary. The fact that a man "is" a Jew is accepted. The deeper meaning is left to the future. Such pragmatic approaches may be dangerous and lead to superficiality. There is no doubt that the search for the deeper meaning of Jewish existence will be the most important item on the agenda of Jewish living in the future. It is beginning to disturb the younger generation, which is deeply dissatisfied with the vulgarity of the Jewish world of *Marjorie Morningstar*, and finds small comfort in the emotional thrills of *Exodus*.

For the first time in Jewish history the Jews live in a country which takes the separation of church and state more seriously than any other country in the world. When we speak of American freedom, we must define it clearly within its own framework, which has no parallel in the world. All such great concepts as freedom are subject to concrete clarification in a time when words are proudly proclaimed in all countries, and when the same words used in England, France, the Soviet Union and the United States mean something quite different in any one of them. The great and decisive battle against the slightest infringement upon the principle of separation of church and state is a purely American battle. For the Jews, this is a completely new experience. In countries of persecution, such as Russia, the government interfered even with their religious life. It meddled in matters of deep convictions. It imposed Liberal Judaism on Orthodox Jews and forbade the beard and the "Jewish" dress. In Prussia, the government, at least at the beginning of the Emancipation, sat in judgment over what was authentic Judaism. In Germany, Jews levied taxes upon the members of their community which were collected by the state. To leave the organized Jewish community and live as an unaffiliated Jew required a declaration before the State Court. In most countries of Europe, including France, England, Holland, Austria, Hungary, Scandinavia and Germany, religious Jewish (and Christian) training was provided and paid for by the state in state-financed public schools. In many of these countries the rabbis were paid by the state, and chief rabbis appointed by the Jewish community with the approval of the state authorities often occupied official positions in the governmental families.

To be a Jew in the United States under the specific freedom which is spelled out in the American idea, and lived in accordance with the mores of the country, is radically different from anything which the Jews ever experienced. To be a Jew means to have chosen to be part of a specific group. The association with that group is a voluntary and therefore a moral act. There is no governmental decree, no law, no Pale of Settlement that might make such a decision or such choice necessary. In the course of our examination we shall look a bit more closely into this freedom of choice. We shall discover that some qualifications will be necessary. As the "life, liberty and the pursuit of happiness" of the American Constitution suffers some loss of luster in the process of the translation of these "eternal" values into the reality of daily life, so is the "freedom" under which the decision to be a Jew is made a qualified freedom. Nevertheless, we have reasons to believe that were it even closer to the great concept of "justice and liberty for all," the voluntary decision of the majority of American Jews would be for the group to which they belong because they like it.

"Because they like it" is perhaps not a very glorious affirmation. But it is infinitely more honest than the laborious approach of those who try to "justify" their Jewish allegiance with their pride of belonging to a people who wrote the Bible and produced so many Einsteins. It is an affirmation of one's self, and there is no firmer and more wholesome identification than this. Martin Buber, in one of his as yet untranslated essays on the problem of the contemporary Jew, reduces the complicated political and social problems of the Jew to this self-discovery of the Jew.

"The Jewish problem," he says, "is not at all political. What a Jew, marooned on an island and looking into his innermost self, discovers to be his Jewishness — this and this alone is the Jewish problem." The American Jew has looked into himself. He has discovered that being a Jew is profoundly a part of his very being. He would probably be hard put to explain it in rational terms. Nor does this discovery have any consequences in either religious or organizational terms. But I doubt that there are many Jews in America today who would find any pleasure and satisfaction in hiding the fact that they are Jews. Even in the interesting, and often alarming, confessions of Jewish intellectuals undertaken by a national magazine, none of them expresses any doubt about that. More ambitious or impatient people might find this unsatisfactory, and would like to probe more deeply into the consequences of such Jewish self-affirmation. But to me, the self-affirmation of the American Jew, however far removed it may be from Jewish convictions or participation in Jewish life, is an eminently important beginning. It is a far cry from the attitude of the Jewish intellectuals in Europe who, like Henri Bergson, Max Scheler and countless others, converted to Christianity and — in some cases — to Jewish self-hatred. I say it is a good beginning, not more and not less. This attitude is new in a setting of complete acculturation. It is typical of the special case that is

American Jewry. It may not at all or only partly be due to the new Jewish climate of the post-Hitler and post-Zionist period. But it is also deeply embedded in the structure of a new American society.

The question is whether the spirit of conformity and egalitarianism will not, in the end, liquidate every separate group in America, including, of course, the Jews. It is a long time since Horace Kallen and others began to reject the concept of the American "melting pot," and advanced the new idea of "cultural pluralism." Since he and his like-minded philosopher-sociologists were pragmatists, the new theory was not prompted by idealistic notions. It was the result of keen observation of the American reality of the twentieth century. Kallen writes: "The United States is no more, and no less, a melting pot than any other country in the world. Italians and Jews and Yankees and Irishmen may have become people of a single culture, tradition, aspiration and public behavior, yet *they will regularly associate with people of their own racial and familial tone, and their marriages will not so very largely overflow the boundaries set by these factors and their churches. The United States is conspicuously marked by groupings of this kind.*" * These "groupings" are a fact of American life. The Jews are but one of many such groups.

* Horace Kallen, *Culture and Democracy in the United States*, p. 184.

No longer is the problem assimilation *or* group survival. This alternative, so very real in the nineteenth century, is both a simplification of the problem and an inaccurate interpretation of the American realities. Nor is the problem merely a Jewish one. There are few ethnic groups in America today, the America of the third and fourth generation, which are not fully "acculturated," to use the term of the social scientists. But acculturation, that is, a group's undoubted identification with everything that is American in habit, politics, language, mores, idiosyncrasies, patriotism, provincialism, and the rest of it, does not in any way impair the continued existence of the ethnic group with its own set of values, social, religious and otherwise. If assimilation is to mean disintegration of a group, it has become unrealistic to debate it. It is important to understand this, for the international Jewish debate about American Jewry and its future continues to emphasize the problems of "assimilation," as though America of the twentieth century were France or Germany of the nineteenth. Even those countries have changed, albeit for other reasons. The very nature of America as the classic country of immigrants tends toward preserving its character as "one nation, indivisible, with liberty and justice *for all,*" meaning that all groups, each of them adhering to its own heritage, enjoy freedom, and in their separateness, form this "indivisible nation." There is no need and indeed no desire for conformity to a fictitious "majority" pattern.

This then is a new situation, incomparably new, in both the history of societies and certainly in the historic experience of the Jews. The American society, which is the result of many waves of migrations, has nothing in common with those nations in Europe which have not changed in centuries and whose immigrants had been absorbed hundreds of years before the modern states came into being. Neither in France nor in any other Western country was there a population structure comparable to the United States. The Austrian-Hungarian monarchy, which contained a large number of "minorities" living in clearly defined geographic areas, never conceived of the idea of cultural and political amalgamation. It was in reality a federation of states, each of which constituted a national entity with political aspirations often inimical to those of the state, a situation so complicated that it was bound to lead to the final collapse in 1918. The Jews had their own particular status in each of the states, and were even represented as a national group in the national Parliament. The other European countries had no need for any cultural pluralism because of their unitarian character. The Jews, as we have seen, presented a problem before and after their Emancipation, but it can in no way be compared with the American situation.

It is also important to note that nowhere (outside the East European countries, where the situation was totally different) did the Jews constitute a very large group. More often than not, their number was well under 3 per cent, and even under 1 per cent of the entire population. Vienna and Berlin never had more than 180,000 Jews; Budapest never more than 250,000. Compare this with New York's more than two million Jews! But we are not dealing here with mere statistics. The large, unparalleled concentration of Jews is one of the great safety factors, one which renders every one of the European analyses of the "Jewish problem" utterly inaccurate and useless. Jews live in the United States within Jewish communities so large as to provide for the individual Jew every conceivable satisfaction of his needs. The Jewish community provides jobs for Jews within a Jewish sector which has its limitations, to be sure, but which absorbs those Jews who would not find jobs elsewhere. There are large areas of economic pursuits to which Jews are attracted because they can be sure of employment. This does not eliminate, nor does it minimize, the existence of discrimination in banking, heavy industry, and insurance companies, which have always adhered to a policy of not hiring Jews for their top positions. But although nobody would suggest that such practices should not be checked by legislation wherever possible, they do not constitute a Jewish problem. Those thousands of young people, professionals and businessmen who were without work and hope in anti-Semitic Poland and Rumania in the thirties do not exist in the United States. There are no statistics relating to unemployment resulting from discrimination. But American Jewry is prosperous, and unemployment is not one of its problems unless it becomes the problem of the entire middle class.

The satisfaction of the needs of American Jewry which is provided by the large numbers, concentrated in a few urban centers, is not merely economic. It has important social implications. In a society which creates large areas of commercial and professional interplay and cooperation among all groups, the after-work hours are left to social life within the group. Acculturation in the widest sense, which includes integration in commerce, political activities, professional and scientific pursuits, and every other possible activity, does not necessarily mean the sharing of the intimate relationship of family, worship, love, leisure hours, country club, social intercourse and all the other forms of "after-six-o'clock" life. It is there that the indiscriminate "togetherness" gives way to group life. This is true not only of the Jews. The role of church and synagogue in America is not merely one of an institution which stands for clearly defined religious convictions. As a matter of fact, this is one of the problems of both Christianity and Judaism, whose leaders would like to cultivate and emphasize convictions, pure and simple, and are confronted with the task of providing social facilities for their respective groups instead. And this is true not merely of the organized religions; it is true of all the other social agencies, in the fields of welfare, supplementary education and relaxation. It is difficult for Europeans to understand this American phenomenon in terms other than those of group tensions. But it is not that easy. Nobody, of course, will deny the existence of a scale of social acceptability. Each of the groups has its own social status. But this is not the only reason for a social separation which is almost complete. It is true that Jews and others formed their own country clubs and social outlets because they were not admitted to others, and there is no doubt that the generation of the twenties felt it as a rebuff, but I doubt whether this is valid any longer. There is less awareness and certainly much less soreness about nonadmission into the socially preferable club or group. There are today practically no attempts to "penetrate" into those forbidden gardens. There is an acceptance of the social facts which are characteristic of the American society, and hardly any attempt is made to fight them. There is no neurosis resulting from it, save in some extraordinary cases. Louis Wirth, in his book *The Ghetto,* quotes from the manuscript of "A Jewish College Man":

"I graduated with the highest honors from the medical school. Of course in my college career I felt somewhat out of the run of things because there were certain fraternities that some friends of mine belonged to that never asked a Jew to join. But I took that gracefully. I said to myself, 'They have a long tradition against admitting Jews, but as individuals they are quite friendly to me, and I'm sure they would ask me to join if it weren't for the rules, for which they are not to blame.'

"Of course I never hid the fact that I was a Jew, although I may say that my appearance would never betray my race. I said to myself, as I looked at all of the ghetto boys in school: 'I don't blame them for being prejudiced. Look at them, with their outlandish ways, their mannerisms, their unmitigated nerve and forwardness. Who wouldn't be ashamed to be a Jew? Under circumstances like that, who blames the fraternities for not taking them in? They can't be just an ordinary member of anything. They've got to run the thing or ruin it.'

"Secretly I sympathized with the feeling against the Jews, and I decided that as for myself, while I would never renounce my people, I would try to make myself worthy of the friendship of Gentiles. I sometimes argued with these Russian Jews (I was German myself, American-born), and told them that if they didn't make themselves so conspicuous and obnoxious the rest of the Jews would stand a chance. But they told me that I would find out soon enough that there were no exceptions, that to the Gentiles a

Jew was a Jew whether he had blond hair or dark hair, and that they could smell them a mile away.

"I got into my profession and worked in an office where there was one prominent Jewish specialist who was respected by all of his colleagues. There was a model Jew — quiet, dignified, inconspicuous. I would emulate him. Once a Gentile friend in the profession asked me whether I didn't want to join a club he belonged to. I didn't know much about it, but I liked him and wanted to be a good sport. I said I would join. A couple of weeks later he met me rather shamefacedly and said, 'You know I'm sorry, old pal, they found out you were a Jew and there is a rule against admitting Jews. It's a disgusting arrangement. I've decided to resign my membership.' I calmed him and told him not to go to the trouble, that if I had known it would cause him any trouble I would have told him so to begin with, but I didn't know that they excluded Jews. It didn't interfere with my friendship with him, but it caused me a lot of mental anguish.

"I brooded over the thing, and concluded that you simply couldn't escape it. There are only two ways out: One is to stand up and fight back like a man, and I didn't have the courage to do that singlehanded, and didn't like to join the kind of bunch that is doing the fighting, because I think they make the thing worse than it is. The other is to go right on brooding over your lot, and join the B'nai B'rith and become a Zionist and join the Jewish clubs and the temple, and let the world take its course. I say I didn't have the courage for the first, and had no inclination for the

latter, so here I am — nobody, a dual personality —
a man with two souls, a man without a country." *

But, characteristically, this book was written in
1928. I doubt very much that the same college man
would write it in 1962. There is a new Jewish self-
respect which would prevent Jewish men and women
in or out of college from denigrating themselves by
submitting applications in places where they would
be merely tolerated. The fact of the matter is that the
mood and attitudes of the American Jews have
changed. The dominant attitude now is that it is
good to be with like-minded people of similar background and that scales of social status set up by the
majority group need not be accepted as valid.

Even in dealing with anti-Semitism, the approach
has changed from that of the nineteenth century and
even from that of twenty years ago. New insights of
social science and the experience of the Hitler era
have had their decided influence. Nobody has any illusions about the existence of prejudice or about our
ability to remove it. The whole area of the irrational,
the unfathomable, the unconscious and the subconscious, so foreign to the rationalists of a generation
ago, has become an integral part of our intellectual
pattern. No longer do Jews think of anti-Semitism as a
combatable, arguable, rational proposition. They understand that there is no room for arguments where

* Louis Wirth, *The Ghetto,* p. 266.

blind rejection, prejudices or even hatred motivate human behavior. They have begun to understand that the attack must not be on *prejudice* but on *discrimination,* and that the battle against discrimination can and must be fought in a democracy. This battle might be difficult, but there is a good chance that it can be won. Yet anti-Jewish discrimination, in spite of the very specific nature of anti-Semitic prejudice, cannot be fought as an isolated, purely Jewish battle. It must be part of the great, historic effort to bring America closer to self-fulfillment, and to achieve equality of rights for all its peoples. This approach is now accepted by all of organized American Jewry. The last decade has shown how much can be achieved through legislation which includes all minority groups, people of many races and creeds. While other Jewries are still concerned with anti-Semitic incidents, American Jews have gained a new perspective, new moral strength and much hope in the common front for the battle to end all discrimination in education, housing and employment. Very few other undertakings have brought so many Americans of various backgrounds together. None has afforded them a better opportunity to know and to respect each other. The old European Jewish attempts to "fight anti-Semitism" as a purely Jewish enterprise which failed so tragically in Germany and Austria seem outmoded and ineffective; they lack the moral strength which is part of our prophetic tradition that bids us to "pursue justice" for all people. These convictions have removed fear from the hearts of American Jews. There is no longer any trembling in the face of the few lunatic groups who preach hatred. Never in the history of the United States has the government favored anti-Semitic acts. No law has been promulgated that excluded Jews from any part of public life. Never once has the President of the United States or any other responsible member of the government permitted himself to make a single anti-Semitic utterance. Nor would a political party be so ludicrous as to make anti-Semitic discrimination a part of its platform. All this was quite different in Europe. Political parties in France, Germany, Austria, Romania and Hungary have not hesitated to urge anti-Semitic legislation upon their governments, and many such parties — long before Hitler — were elected *because* of their anti-Semitism. No objective observer of the political scene in Germany was surprised to see Hitler come to power. There was enough historical precedence for both organized anti-Semitism and dictatorship in that country. Of course, the events which took place under the Hitler regime have caused people to think that "it can happen here," too. The change of public mood, the lack of civil courage, the vulgarization of public debate, the onslaught on the integrity of human rights during the McCarthy episode have put some doubts into the minds of the overconfident. The shrill, hysterical voices of American mothers who jeered at little Negro children entering the schools in Little Rock and New Orleans, the attacks upon the Freedom Riders have confirmed the contention of those who believe that all people, including Americans, are capable of mob brutality and injustices. Nobody can afford to be complacent about the potential for dictatorship, the rule of the mob and the betrayal of human decency even in America. But it must be added that if it were to happen, it would no longer be a problem for minorities, Jewish or otherwise. It would be a problem for all of America and indeed for the world. It is difficult to conceive of such radical changes in the whole system of the American government and in the national character of the American people. The United States of America, as it is constituted today, and the people of America as a collective entity are as safe a guarantee for the unmolested future of the Jewish people as exists anywhere in the world.

This analysis of the special situation of American Jewry would be incomplete if we were not to mention one decisive historic fact: there was never a Declaration of Emancipation for the Jews of America. They are not citizens now because of any special right or decree. They are citizens because they live in this country, and have earned this right by either birth or personal declaration of intention to become citizens.

There was never a time when Jews were not citizens. Since 1789 they have lived under the Constitution, which guaranteed them the rights of citizens. Any attempt to compare the Jewish experience in Europe with the Jewish situation in America must take this into account. Rights which were never specially granted cannot be repealed. The Jew is as much of a stranger as is the Irishman, the Swede or the German, or for that matter, any other American. There is no memory of an American Middle Ages when Jews were herded into ghettos, when they wore the yellow badge, and from which they had to be "liberated" by the social and political upheavals of the eighteenth and nineteenth centuries. These facts are largely overlooked in the protracted discussion between European and Israeli Jewry and American Jewry.

The cultural and political adjustment which the Jewish immigrant has made, and which is now taken for granted by his children and grandchildren, has not resulted in any organized attempt to lose the Jewish sense of identity. And this "sense of identity" is not merely a group instinct. Horace Kallen writes:

> They [the Jews] come from lands of sojourn where they have for ages been treated as foreigners, at most as semi-citizens, subject to disabilities and persecutions. They come with no political aspirations against the peace of other states such as move the Irish, the Poles, the Bohemians. They come with the intention

to be completely incorporated into the body-politic of the state. They alone, as Mr. H. G. Wells notes, of all the immigrant people have made spontaneous conscious and organized efforts to prepare themselves and their brethren for the responsibilities of American citizenship. There is hardly a considerable municipality in the land, where Jews inhabit, that has not its Hebrew Institute or its Educational Alliance, or its Young Men's Hebrew Association, or its Community House, especially dedicated to this task. . . . Yet of all group-conscious peoples they are the most group-conscious. Of all immigrants they have the oldest civilized tradition, they are longest accustomed to living under law, and are at the outset the most eager and the most successful in eliminating the removable differences between themselves and their social environment. Even their religion is flexible and accommodating as that of the Christian sectaries is not, for change involves no change in doctrine, only in mode of life. Yet — once the wolf is driven from the door and the Jewish immigrant takes his place in American society a free man (as American *mores* establish freedom) and an American, he tends to become rather the more a Jew. The cultural unity of his race, history and background, is only continued by the new life under the new conditions. Mr. H. G. Wells calls the Jewish quarter in New York a city within a city, and more correctly than other quarters because, although it is far more in tune with Americanism than the other quarters, it is also far more autonomous in spirit and self-conscious in culture. It has had its sectaries, its radicals, its artists, its literati; its press, its literature, its theatre, its Yiddish and its Hebrew, its Talmudical Colleges and its Hebrew Schools, its charities and its vanities, and its coordinating organization, the Kehilla, all more or less reduplicated wherever Jews congregate in mass. Here not religion alone, but the whole world of liberated thinking carries the mother tongue and the father tongue, with all that they imply.*

The analysts of the Jewish problem in the "assimilated" communities of the nineteenth century have pointed to two major manifestations of the corroding process which would inevitably destroy the cohesiveness of the Jewish community: conversion and intermarriage. There were good reasons to be worried about them. Since the early days of the Emancipation, conversion was the surest way out of the Jewish dilemma. And ever since Heinrich Heine, himself a convert, had called the conversion to Christianity an "admission ticket to European civilization," it became the clearest proof of Jewish degeneration. The perfunctory nature of such conversions of convenience was well known to both the Christian clergy and the Jews themselves. Countless jokes, most of them circulated by Jews, made the rounds and seemed to make light of what had become one of the real threats to Jewish existence. There was indeed no better way to

* Horace Kallen, *Culture and Democracy in the United States,* p. 111.

make certain that at least the children and the grand-children would not suffer any discrimination. No-body could have foreseen that conversion would not protect a person under the Hitler regime, and that there was no security even for the grandchildren. In a more civilized era, conversion was heartily recom-mended and warmly applauded. It opened many doors, both in the universities and in the army. No wonder that hundreds of thousands of Jews took advantage of this new opportunity. It is generally agreed that the figure of 224,000 for converts in the nineteenth century (as estimated by the Protestant clergyman Johan de le Roi) is too low. But even if we accept this figure for want of a more accurate one, it seems clear that the Jews were confronted with a formidable problem. It is no wonder that Jewish leaders were deeply alarmed by the ever growing number of con-verts in all European countries, including Russia. The list of converted Jews reads like *Who's Who* in the arts, the sciences and literature. If a man bearing a Jewish name had been appointed to a full professor-ship at any European university during the nine-teenth and even at the beginning of the twentieth cen-tury, it was taken for granted that he was a converted Jew.

The problem of intermarriage was even more severe. It would have led to the complete destruction of the Jewish communities of Central Europe, as it has continued to decimate the small Jewish communities of Scandinavia. The figures are appalling: Between 1900 and 1924, 103,000 Jewish weddings took place in Germany. During the same period of time, 33,800 mixed marriages were concluded. While the rate of intermarriage in Prussia was only 4.4 per cent in 1876, it had risen to 25 per cent in 1927. In some cities the percentages were even higher: in Berlin (1923) 27 per cent, in Hamburg (1924) 71 per cent, in Budapest (1927) 33 per cent; and in Magdeburg the mixed marriages exceed the Jewish ones by 25 per cent (against 100 purely Jewish marriages, there were 125 mixed marriages between 1925 and 1927). The figures for the years immediately preceding the Hitler regime are not available. If they were, they would show a considerable increase. It was easy for a Jewish sociologist in Germany to predict in 1911 that German Jewry would simply disappear. He was not prophesying the coming of Hitler. He was referring to conversion and intermarriage.

These figures must be borne in mind if we now return to American Jewry. Conversion — though it occurs in a few individual cases — is no problem at all. We find attempts to join the more "palatable" churches — the Unitarians or the Ethical Culture societies, and sometimes the Christian Science Church. But these religious "convictions" are rarely handed down to the next generation. Since those Jews remain Jews in terms of their social associations, the attempt at conversion rarely succeeds. It is altogether sporadic and restricted to small groups. Intermarriage, which loomed so large in the European analysis of the Jewish situation and which seemed such a natural by-product of social adjustments, remains a surprisingly insignificant fact in American Jewish life. The statistics published in 1957 by the United States Census study of religion reported the Jewish percentage of mixed marriages to be the smallest of any religious group; while 8.6 per cent of all Protestants were married to non-Protestants and 21.6 per cent of all Catholics to non-Catholics, the figure for the Jews was a mere 7.2 per cent. Nor is this merely true of the Jews of the United States. It is equally valid in Canada, where 245,000 Jews live, a dynamic Jewish community, in many respects much more "Jewish" than its American counterpart. The situation in England is slightly different, although the similarities in all Anglo-Saxon countries, including Australia and South Africa, are close enough to permit us to apply our analysis of the American Jewish scene.

Paradoxically, one of the main problems of American Jewry lies in its structure. The group structure of America is a guarantor of Jewish group survival, as we have seen. There is no doubt that Jews will continue to exist and that the European problems of disintegration which stirred Zionism into action are

not applicable to American Jewry. Whether the group
structure was originally stimulated by anti-Semitism or
by the desire of immigrants to live in Jewish neighborhoods is immaterial. The fact remains that in America
Jews live together; some of the neighborhoods have
been called "gilded ghettos." Doubtless in sociological
terminology such neighborhoods with a compact Jewish or other ethnic group could be called that. But
the factor of pressure and persecution is absent, and
this is a very important factor. Living together, however, has become a fact, and whether or not Jews looking for living quarters of any description (high-priced
or middle-class) actually ask for such a neighborhood,
they usually (at least in areas of large Jewish popu-
lations) find themselves surrounded by Jewish neighbors. Where they do not find Jewish next-door neighbors, they will soon discover that their social life is
nevertheless "Jewish." This does not exclude a cor-
dial and even warm relationship with Christian neighbors. It, of course, does not exclude cases of genuine
friendships between Jews and Christians. They exist,
particularly at the universities, among artists, and at
times even among businessmen. But they are rare.
They are rare, not because of anti-Semitism, but because of the American principle of social homogene-
ity. Some people might deny this and claim that it is
anti-Semitism, pure and simple. It cannot be denied
that some polls taken indicate that the social status

of the Jews is not as high as that of a white Episcopalian New Englander. But if this be so, it is a peculiar form of prejudice. In a public-opinion poll taken one year after the election of President John F. Kennedy, the question was asked whether people would vote for a Jewish candidate for the presidency if he were qualified. Of the total number, 72 per cent said they would. This would be impossible in an anti-Semitic society. Two Jews now serve with great distinction as members of the Cabinet. Many of them occupy high governmental positions. The group structure is not restricted to Jews. It is the pattern of American living.

It is this group structure which makes American Jewry a unique phenomenon and renders most European approaches to America's Jewish "problem" inadequate. It is true that this very group structure, in which there is so much safety for collective survival, might create social claustrophobia. There is no way out. It assumes, at times, comical forms. Jews who don't like to be Jews associate and even live with likeminded negativists. In Jerome Weidman's *Enemy Camp*, an intermarried couple moving to Westchester County looks for other couples in the neighborhood who have similar problems, and they find them. There are, however, not merely comical aspects. There is great danger in any group and ghetto living. Habits develop in both speech and outlook which make it difficult for many people to adjust in a world without

Jews. Jewish boys who leave their protective ghetto to serve in the armed forces or to attend college have found these adjustments difficult and at times painful. Very often they leave a home community which had provided a school experience with a Jewish majority in public school. Ghetto habits are always bad habits because they often include ghetto mentality. Although there are no walls, life in the Jewish neighborhood with sociability centered around Jewish homes or Jewish organizations is bound to have its effect and create a parochial outlook. Political opinions are formed within this compact social group which tend to prevent an objective appraisal of political opinion "outside" the ghetto. These negative aspects must not be overlooked. But they do not militate against Jewish survival. They may be deplored and indeed be deplorable. But our problem of continued Jewish existence in America is not affected by it.

However, there are other shortcomings which need attention. Far from resenting this Jewish group life, most American Jews find it comfortable to live "amongst their own people." They feel socially ill at ease with others. With their own people, they have a whole world of interests in common. They have mutual friends. But the satisfaction is not merely social. It has certain connotations in terms of our concern for Jewish survival. Their conscience is pacified. There is little chance that they might lose their identity, because assimilation has become physically impossible. The group structure protects the group identity. It is a mechanical process. Nothing has to be done to survive. And physical group survival assuages all guilt feelings which would arise if this were not so. As long as the group exists, nobody needs to worry about the *meaning* of this survival. It is self-perpetuating. It requires neither thought nor work. It is a fact of life.

But survival, if it is properly understood, is not merely a fact of life. Inbreeding may cause perpetual survival of the group, but what sense is there in preserving a group unless the group is preserved for a purpose? It is true that physical survival is meaningful in the face of pogroms which threaten to hurt and kill. It was most meaningful in concentration camps and in Russia's Pale of Settlement. It makes sense even in the face of an anti-Semitic movement which threatens the very existence of the Jewish community. All these considerations do not apply to America. Here the Jew lives in a democratic society. He is free. It is this very freedom that poses the problem. The "to be or not to be" problem is not the American Jewish dilemma. The Jews "are." They exist. But is existence the whole purpose of living as a Jew? Can it indeed be that Jews should maintain themselves as a distinct group only for the purpose of being a distinct group? It is good to be different, for differences, to the sophisticated and brave, are added value. Conformity is not. But is this "difference" of sufficient value to warrant its preservation? It is the question of value with which we are concerned. The term "survival" conveys merely the desire to survive. It does not spell out that the concern is with the creative continuity of Jewish values, whatever they may be. Such continuity of Jewish values, however, is not guaranteed by mere existence. It is not produced by the magic of Jewish sociability. It needs a concerted, thoughtful effort. It calls for definitions, thought, ideas and a plan for action. Our problem, therefore, is freedom. Freedom for what purpose? Freedom is an untested Jewish experience. We have never survived under freedom, either because there never was uninterrupted freedom or — as in the case of Scandinavian Jewry — we succumbed. The era of the first freedom between the French Revolution and Hitler was a period of assimilation. The American situation does not permit that kind of group disintegration. But does this sense of security solve the problem of meaningful Jewish existence in a democracy? Strange and paradoxical as it may seem, our problem is: Can we survive *in spite* of freedom and democracy?

Never has such a painful problem existed in another Jewish community. For freedom is one of the great values in a world of bondage and autocracy. And democracy is almost a religious term in this world of rivaling ideologies. Our very question therefore sounds like high treason committed against the most deeply cherished values of our time. Yet it might be comforting to know that the uses to which freedom must be put are in reality the most important problem of the free world itself. There, too, the value of freedom must be tested if we are to survive. In the case of the Jew, freedom must not be abused for comfortable living. It must be used to perpetuate not merely the group, but the purposes which have made Jewish existence a meaningful and even important experience for mankind. Jewish survival in terms of existence is an egotistical enterprise benefiting only those who want to live and enjoy living. Creative Jewish continuity may be painful and difficult. It will, however, have its profound effect on the Jewish people and the world. Its importance is not parochial. It is a problem of the preservation of the Jewish spirit, which has impressed itself upon humanity and its civilization. Group preservation and universality are not at all mutually exclusive. The great creations in art, literature and religion came from a small, well-defined, often even geographically confined group. Homer lived on his island and Rembrandt in Amsterdam. Religious creativity does not occur in a vacuum. It is bound to receive its special color and spirit from specific peoples and landscapes: Buddhism is genuine and pure only in Asia. Spanish Catholicism differs from Polish Catholicism. Nothing great has ever been written in Esperanto, "everybody's language." Everybody's language is in reality nobody's language. The great works of world literature have been written in Greek, Hebrew, English, and obscure languages of the North. Being oneself and affirming it is the prerequisite of creativity. This is true for any kind of creative living. It is also true for the Jews. A discussion of Jewish creative survival under freedom must take this into serious consideration.

There will be some who will maintain that this whole discussion is nonsensical. The Jews, they will claim, live in the United States and elsewhere (outside of Israel) as a religious group, and there is nothing more to the discussion than the problem of Judaism as a faith and the religious validity of Jewish religious tenets in the twentieth century. There are, the argument continues, three religious bodies in America: Catholics, Protestants and Jews. Each of them has its own cult, its own houses of worship, its own set of rules. Judaism must therefore conform to this pattern, which is generally accepted, and all other problems exist only in the minds of Jewish nationalists. Jews, they contend, are Americans of the Jewish faith. It's as simple as that.

But nothing that concerns the Jews is simple. The very fact that they *exist* seems anomalous. They should have disappeared long ago, together with the Babylonians, the Assyrians and the Hittites. Yet they did not. Against all rules of statistical calculations and every single law of history, they continue to exist. In spite of their own dire prophecies, they merge into each new era of world history, indestructible notwithstanding the pogroms, gas chambers and every conceivable form of cruelty. Indeed, the thousand catastrophes which have befallen them since their exodus from Egypt seem to arouse them to new vitality. It would be easy to write Jewish history as a history of calamities. It would be more accurate and much more worthwhile to write it in terms of the most astounding creative use to which they put every single catastrophe, and in terms of their national and spiritual resilience which follows death and destruction. There is actually no ready term in the political or sociological vocabulary to explain the strange fact of Jewish survival, nor any easy way to cope with it. Even the usual categories which place groups into various rubrics prove fruitless in the case of the Jews. What are they really? A nation? A strange nation indeed, scattered over the globe with no language of their own, no country and no government. Never in their long history did they leave a country voluntarily. The legend of the wandering Jew is one of the many distortions of Jewish history.

Contrary to popular belief, viciously or inadvertently nourished by legend and fairy tales, the Jews are not at all given to wanderlust, a people without roots. With unbelievable tenacity, the Jews clung to the country which had permitted them to settle; and if they had to leave, they did so at the last possible moment. Very often they missed the last boat, or the last train. This accounts for the many victims. The German Jews, for instance, died in such large numbers because they did not take Hitler seriously. How could anybody deny them their right to live in a country in which they had made their home for sixteen hundred years? Many fled to Holland and France, and called it security. So much irrationality cannot be due to mere miscalculation of political realities, but to an almost unbelievable romantic relationship to the country of their birth.

These Jews, thought to be shrewd, calculating and down-to-earth, were, in reality, sentimentalists. Their history is not one of migrations, but one of expulsions. But when they settle in the new country, they sink their roots deep into the soil. There is something naïve, something touching, in their romantic love for the countries in which they have lived. They came to Babylon in 586 B.C. after the fall of Jerusalem, were herded together and led into what the Babylonians thought was captivity. The prisoners found it difficult "to sing the songs of Zion on foreign soil." But their children sang the songs of Babylon. The rivers of Babylon which caused their parents to weep became streams of joy and laughter to their offspring. When less than sixty years later Cyrus of Persia, in his version of the Balfour Declaration, gave them permission to leave for Jerusalem, less than 10 per cent of them took advantage of it, and many of them were "professional Jews." Babylon had become their home, and they stayed on. Not without concern for the people in the Holy Land, and not without developing an admirable Jewish creativity. But they stayed on.

When they were forced to leave Palestine, their homeland, at the time of the burning of the Second Temple, the prisoners marched down the alley of victory in Rome, and settled all over the world: in Rome itself, in Spain, on the Aegean Islands, in North Africa, in Egypt and many other countries — and they stayed on for thousands of years. The German Jews, for example, settled in Cologne in the wake of the Roman military occupation. They built their synagogue in 321 (the ruins were uncovered during the bombing of Cologne) and stayed there almost uninterruptedly until Hitler drove them out.

The Jews of Russia, who were treated so badly that they did not become citizens of Russia until 1917, who were never permitted into the large cities and were restricted to a Pale of Settlement and subjected to pogrom after pogrom, carried Russia with them wherever they went and spoke nostalgically about it. Much of what is considered "Jewish food" is in reality Russian national dishes: gefilte fish, stuffed cabbage, borscht and rye bread. What is commonly considered

"Jewish" music is to all intents and purposes Russian.

What is true of food and music is doubly true of language. In the late Middle Ages, when the Jews were forced to leave Germany and settled in the east of Europe, they took their language with them. This may be true of all immigrants. The first generation speaks the language of the "old country." The children still understand it, and the grandchildren forget all about it. Not so the Jews. They took their medieval German, together with the costume of the German peasant, the twisted bread of the German, and then preserved it for generations until this day, more than four hundred years later. Yiddish is medieval German. Walther von der Vogelweide, the German medieval troubadour, spoke a German much more akin to Yiddish than what his kinsfolk speak today. The Jews expelled from Spain in 1492 took their homeland with them. They settled in Amsterdam, Turkey and upper Italy, but they continued to speak, until this very day, Ladino, the Castilian dialect of fifteenth-century Spain. There are Judeo-Spanish, Judeo-German and Judeo-Arabic, a linguistic phenomenon as unique and unparalleled as the Jews themselves.

But although the Jews carry the old country with them, they adapt to the new country with unbelievable speed. Of all the groups that have come to the United States, Jews have the smallest number of returnees. Between 1915 and 1920, 56.6 per cent of emigrants to the United States returned to their home countries. During that same period, only 4.3 per cent of the Jews returned. The return to their home countries among Jews never exceeded 7 per cent as against 56 per cent in other groups. This is not merely because there was no country to which to return. For centuries Spain has made strenuous efforts to persuade the Jews to return to that country; postwar Germany was very eager for the Jews to come back, and all kinds of monetary inducements were offered to potential returnees, but very few accepted. Most of those who returned were old, and came back to die rather than to "live at home."

If the Jews are not a nation, they certainly are not a race. Physiognomically, Israel is almost a United Nations. All shades of color — from the darkest black of the Abyssinian Falashas, to the olive skin of the Indian, Iraqi and Yemenite Jews, to the light, blond-haired and blue-eyed German and English Jews. Racially, there is no kinship at all. The American Jew who meets Jews in the mellahs of Morocco or Addis Ababa, or even in the Oriental quarter of Israel, has little in common with them other than the knowledge that they are his people.

Are the Jews a faith then? Here, too, the Christian definitions of faith seem to be hopelessly inadequate. For although their creativity found its most enduring expression in the realm of religion, it would be difficult to define Jews merely as members of a faith. Jews have in their long history maintained a most intimate relationship to God and made Him the beginning and the end of things, but their preoccupation was not with faith and dogmas, but with life. Whether Judaism is indeed, as Moses Mendelssohn defined it, a "revealed law" is immaterial. There is no doubt that it evolved a way of life in which God's interpreted word was the regulative principle. But it regulated human life. It has little concern with metaphysics. Some students of religion maintain that Judaism is a religion without theology. They doubt whether a Jewish theology is at all possible. *It* had, at any rate, very little influence upon the development of Jewish religious thought. The Jews are a justice-intoxicated people. It is justice and love for human beings that determines their behavior. Justice and love also yielded the important yardsticks in the interpretation of history. God and faith are very much taken for granted; heaven and hell are never discussed. Nor is there a profound discussion of death and life hereafter in many of the Jewish writings, including the Bible. What counts most is the way of life. As long as man lives "in accordance with His law," he is counted a believer.

One of the great difficulties in understanding "different" cultures is that the very terms which the majority created do not apply. For instance, the term "religion," derived from the ecclesiastic Latin *religio*, has no equivalent in Hebrew. The word *dat* for religion has a connotation of law rather than faith. The Hebrew term for faith, *emunah*, means truth and conviction rather than blind faith. Thomas of Aquino, Kierkegaard and Karl Barth have no organic place in Jewish thinking. *Credo quia absurdum est* (I believe because it is absurd) is impossible in the Jewish context. Jewish mysticism is based upon a strange familiarity with God which emphasizes the fact that the Jew knew Him from the time of Abraham, or the beginning of time. It is almost an acquaintance on a first-name basis. Only if we understand this can we comprehend the argument *on equal terms* which begins with Abraham's famous bargain with God and found its greatest and most profound expression in the bitter dialogues of Job. This dispute with God has not really ended. It is very much alive, and I understand well how difficult it must be to use Protestant terms to define Judaism as a faith. Mordecai Kaplan, the founder of the Reconstructionist movement, has called it a *civilization*. Although one may want to try for a more precise term, it is closer to the meaning than either faith or religion. That the Jews are not merely members of a faith does not mean that they have none. On the contrary. The faith of the pious Jew is strong and deep and abiding. But it is, in many respects, a faith with a sense of humor. This does not come from a lack of respect and reverence for God, but from the close and intimate acquaintance with Him. If a Jew should say there is no God, don't believe him. He cannot be serious.

There is a quality to Jewish humanistic piety which is incomprehensible in terms of other religions. Faith in God and His existence are taken for granted. They are never discussed.

In his book *Psychoanalysis and Religion,* Erich Fromm deals with this "humanistic approach" by quoting the following Talmudic stories:

A number of famous rabbinical scholars disagreed with Rabbi Eliezar's views in regard to a point of ritual law. "Rabbi Eliezar said to them: 'If the law is as I think it is then this tree shall let us know.' Whereupon the tree jumped from its place a hundred yards (others say four hundred yards). His colleagues said to him, 'One does not prove anything from a tree.' He said, 'If I am right then this brook shall let us know.' Whereupon the brook ran upstream. His colleagues said to him, 'One does not prove anything from a brook.' He continued and said, 'If the law is as I think then the walls of this house will tell.' Whereupon the walls began to fall. But Rabbi Joshua shouted at the walls and said, 'If the scholars argue a point of law, what business have you to fall?' So the walls fell no further out of respect for Rabbi Joshua but out of respect for Rabbi Eliezar did not straighten up. And that is the way they still are. Rabbi Eliezar took up the argument again and said, 'If the law is as I think, they shall tell us from heaven.' Whereupon a voice from heaven said, 'What have you against Rabbi Eliezar, because the law is as he says.' Whereupon Rabbi Joshua got up and said, 'It is written in the Bible: The law is not in heaven. What does this mean? According to Rabbi Jirmijahu it means since the Torah has been given on Mount Sinai we no longer pay attention to voices from heaven because it is written: You make your decision according to the majority opinion.' It then happened that Rabbi Nathan [one of the participants in the discussion] met the Prophet Elijah [who had taken a stroll on earth] and he asked the Prophet, 'What did God himself say when we had this discussion?' The Prophet answered, 'God smiled and said, My children have won, my children have won.' "

This story . . . emphasizes the autonomy of man's reason with which even the supernatural voices from heaven cannot interfere. God smiles, man has done what God wanted him to do, he has become his own master, capable and resolved to make his decisions by himself according to rational, democratic methods.

The same humanistic spirit can be found in many stories from the Chassidic folklore of more than a thousand years later. The Chassidic movement was a rebellion of the poor against those who had the monopoly of learning or of money. Their motto was the verse of the Psalms: "Serve God in joy." They emphasized feeling rather than intellectual accomplishment, joy rather than contrition; to them (as to Spinoza) joy was the equivalent of virtue and sadness the equivalent of sin. The following story is characteristic of the humanistic and anti-authoritarian spirit of this religious sect:

A poor tailor came to a Chassidic rabbi the day after the Day of Atonement and said to him, "Yesterday I had an argument with God. I told him, 'Oh God, you have committed sins and I have committed sins. But you have committed grave sins and I have committed sins of no great importance. What have you done? You have separated mothers from their children and permitted people to starve. What have I done? I have sometimes failed to return a piece of cloth to a customer or have not been strict in the observance of the law. But I will tell you, God. I will forgive you your sins and you forgive me mine. Thus we are even.' " Whereupon the Rabbi answered, "You fool! Why did you let him get away that easily? Yesterday you could have forced him to send the Messiah."

This story demonstrates even more drastically than than that of Abraham's argument with God the idea that God must live up to His promises just as man must live up to his. If God fails to put an end to the suffering of man as He has promised, man has the right to challenge Him, in fact to force Him to fulfill his promise. While the two stories quoted here are within the frame of reference of monotheistic religion, the human attitude behind them is profoundly different from that behind Abraham's readiness to sacrifice Isaac or Calvin's glorification of God's dictatorial powers.*

* Erich Fromm, *Psychoanalysis and Religion,* pp. 45-48.

The awareness of man's partnership with God is merely one, and probably the most timid, of the Jewish concepts of the limited omnipotence of God. God's partner sometimes assumes a major role. The mystery and that which is hidden and unknown is left to God. But that which is clearly before us, our life and our tasks, is ours and our children's, and we must do it. God created the earth for people to inhabit it, and to assume as their own burden and responsibility the tensions, the perplexities, the dilemmas, the tragedies, the joys, the potentials, the promises and the fulfillments of life. For there is but one life: the span between cradle and grave. "And after that is nothingness."

Of course, Christianity and Judaism have a vast area of tradition which they share and which forms the foundation of both religions. But whenever the term "Judeo-Christian" is used in the context of the Brotherhood Week mentality, it is distorted. This term refers to the concept of one God and the whole, marvelous, fruitful, creative and original world of prophetic Judaism: universalism; ethical responsibility; the equality of man created in God's image; the respect for man's dignity; the ideals of love, peace and justice; the tradition of the Ten Commandments and the social laws; the protection of the weak, the widow and the orphan; the responsibility toward society; human existence under the law of the "Thou shalt" and the "Thou shalt not." Our common heritage must not be forgotten in our attempt to understand the uniqueness, the color and the special flavor of the Jewish religious concerns. For if there is really very little difference between Judaism and Christianity, what is the *raison d'être* of being a Jew? After all, this is not the nineteenth century, and we are no longer so naïvely rationalistic as to believe that religions can be artificially created. Rationalism has tended to disregard history, and many of the imponderables and inconsistencies which have cropped up. Those Ethical Culture groups of Jews who either do not understand Judaism or are eager to forsake their Jewish identification have not created a single living and livable religious symbol. Such "sophisticated" groups would like to eliminate all differences and combine the basis of all religions into one faith, a boring anthology of everything that is fair and good and true, pure thought and no feeling. The rituals, the customs, the holidays, the old songs — all these disappear, and what remains is an exercise in logic and charity founded on the best reasons, the best motivations and the most limited imaginations.

The denial of the uniqueness of Judaism and the Jew neither explains nor solves any problems. We need to take an honest look at both and accept the ugly and the beautiful, the good and the bad. There need be no apology for the devils, nor bragging about the angels, and no special brief for the in-betweens. Let us therefore without fear and trepidation say: The Jews are neither a race nor a nation nor a faith. They are a historic, social and religious phenomenon *sui generis*.

But Jews shun the idea of being different. They very much want to be like everyone else. Instinctively they know that being different is a great burden to bear. But to the entire world, the Jew is very much a Jew. In the tragic and painful effort to make themselves understood in terms of the majority, the Jews resort to the common *denominations* to which their Christian neighbors are accustomed, and in doing so, simplify and destroy their uniqueness. They also disregard the simple reality that to the Gentiles the Jews remain "different," and no easy explanation will change this fact. It is deeply imbedded in the innermost recesses of the Gentile's mind.

Quite apart from the question of faith, there has developed in our world a human being called a Jew who has made his mark in this world and who bears a particular imprint in his character, his outlook, the peculiar brand of his talent, his wit, his idiosyncrasies, his emotional structure and his mentality. For want of a better term, I submit that there lives today, clearly recognizable, a *Homo judaicus*. I prefer this term because it emphasizes both the Jewishness and the humanity. It is important to make a point of both.

The Jewishness of this *Homo judaicus* penetrates and influences his humanity.

Born of the historic experience of the Jew over a very long period of time, his encounter with God and ghetto, with injustice and slaughter, with books and Talmudic argumentation, with laughter and tragedy, the *Homo judaicus* came into being. He exists today in this and other countries and in this our time, the twentieth century. He is not necessarily either remarkable or pleasant. He comes in all sizes, many colors, all human attitudes; he is quiet and loud-mouthed, smart and stupid, gaudy and simple, rich and poor, dark-haired and blond. He is a Jew. He is different.

The decision to be different must be made first, and it must be a personal decision. Jewish commitment, as any other commitment, is not the result of a mathematical equation. Nor is it the result of such objective investigation as the contribution to world civilization. No Jew becomes personally involved in Jewish life because his people wrote the Bible. He can only become involved if the Bible which his people wrote means something to him personally. Unless a Jew feels himself to be part of the stream of Jewish history, there is no chance of his Jewish survival.

It is then for us to turn to the most complicated and most decisive factor in the enigma of Jewish existence: the role of the Jews in the history of Western man. Our

Western civilization is the product of many influences. The great murals in the caves of France and Africa; the statues of Sumer, Egypt and Greece; the temples of Babylonia and Hellas; the mathematical and astronomical calculations of India and China; the tablets of law from Hammurabi to the Code of Napoleon; the word world of Homer and Dante; the great novels and the great philosophies — all this and much more has touched us and found its way into our civilization. We are indeed indebted to every hand that ever painted, built or wrote, to Rome and Athens, to Heliopolis and Babylon, to Florence and Cambridge. But there was only one real and meaningful encounter with antiquity that reaches into the heart, the mentality, and even the subconscious of modern man. This encounter was with the Jews.

When Frederick the Great, so we are told, turned to his Lutheran pastor for clear proof of the existence of God, the clergyman answered without hesitation: "The Jews, your Majesty." We are not aware of the royal reaction to this astounding reply. But it is quite clear that the preacher did not mean to be evasive. To him the Jews were the only living witnesses to those remote days in antiquity when Abraham discovered the oneness of God, the only witnesses also to the life and death of Jesus of Nazareth. Indeed, however important Plato's Dialogues and Dante's Inferno may be to the educated man, however much we may owe to the Upanishads, they do not compare with the stories of Genesis and the Twenty-third Psalm. The awareness of a cultural heritage is left to the tiny group of intellectuals. The heritage of the Jew lives in some form everywhere in the Christian world. No other book has exerted as much influence as the Jewish Bible, both the Old and the New Testaments. Agamemnon and Clytemnestra have no meaning in the life and thought and dreams of the Christian child. But Abraham and Jacob, Joseph and Moses, Jesus and Paul have meaning. They are all Jews.

Since the days of Alexandria when the Hebrew Bible was translated into Greek, the language, the metaphors, the very spirit of the Bible have permeated every Western language. Thousands of Hebrew phrases live in the English language and have become the proverbs of the common man. That "man does not live by bread alone," that "Thou shalt honor thy father and thy mother" are not merely theological statements heard from Christian pulpits, but are some of the spiritual axioms by which men live. A whole long catalogue of such expressions can be added. They are not the property of the educated few, but of the men, women and children in every home in the Western world. When they say "Amen," they speak Hebrew. And they speak it at moments of great emotional impact. The Twenty-third Psalm has almost lost its meaning and pastoral beauty by the almost daily recitation in school, home and church. The stories of the royal household of King David and the wisdom of King Solomon mean more to the average man than those of Richard III and Charlemagne.

I will not deal with the subtler "infiltration" of the Jewish spirit into our Western world. Here we would have to recount the history of painting and sculpture which has fed on the stories of the Old Testament. From the early Romanesque and Byzantine paintings to the unforgettable canvases of Rembrandt, the faces of Jacob and Isaac, and all the other heroes of the Jewish Bible, stir man's imagination. Michelangelo's "Moses" and Donatello's "David" stand there in Italy, the marble symbols of the Hebrew spirit in our civilization. The Gregorian chant is probably built on Jewish cantillation; the architecture of the church is modeled after Hellenistic synagogues. But, above all, the sense of moral conduct, at least as important to democracy as parliamentary government, has its roots in the Ten Commandments, which a Jew wrote in the land of Canaan some three thousand years ago.

There is one more step which *precedes the act of evaluation*. It is the act of identification with the Jewish people. Since we speak and think of the generation that saw Hitler come, conquer, kill and die, this should not be difficult. The identification with the Jewish people in the world is neither a mystical act nor a chauvinistic one. It is quite natural that we should have a bond of common interest and a deep concern with our people in the world. It is ridiculous to expect that an American Jew should identify himself completely with a black Falasha from Ethiopia or a Berberian Jew from the Sahara. But that there is such a people, which has survived the burning of the Temples, the evictions and expulsions, the rapings and the pillagings, the revolutions and the wars and still remains a people, is something of great value to us. A Jew who discovers no identity within himself, with his people as they lived yesterday and as they live today, will not be interested in Jewish survival. This is the prerequisite, and there is no substitute for it. We can write a thousand books on Jewish values or customs and light all the candles in the world, it will avail us little, for the first consideration is the Jew vis-à-vis himself. In this deeply *autobiographical* process, nobody can help. Nor is this always or even often the result of a complicated, self-analytical undertaking. With most people it is quite natural. But some Jews hate to be Jews. There is no cure for them unless a cure is undertaken for all the other neuroses from which they suffer. Self-hatred is a serious matter; but it is a psychiatric, not a Jewish, concern.

To Jews who find peace and comfort in the fact that they are what they are and that they like what they are, the act of self-affirmation is as simple as being born. It needs no special argument, no high-sounding proclamation.

Jewish peoplehood then is no longer the bone of contention that it was in the nineteenth century. It has become clear, even to the most stubborn Jewish isolationist, that it has not helped us to claim that we are not a people. We were treated as such and we know in our own hearts that we are. How can we possibly deny the bonds of common history, common fate and common faith with the millions of Jews scattered all over the globe? How can we in good conscience claim to have no responsibility toward them in their struggle for survival, both physical and spiritual? We are no longer afraid of anti-Semites who talk of "international Jewry." It is an ancient Jewish warning not to mind "what the pagans say." If we speak of Jewish survival, we speak of the continued existence of the whole Jewish people, not an isolated Jewish community. Enough of us have died. Let not Jewish isolationists deprive us of the remnant of the Jewish people wherever they may be, however estranged they may have become from us. Yet Jewish isolationism is one of the real problems in American Jewish life. There are enough voices which claim that our only bonds with world Jewry are humanitarian. This was the attitude of many assimilated Jews in Central Europe to whom East European Jews were foreigners in need of charity. When they met them later it was as fellow-inmates in concentration camps. If the Jewish people will survive, it will survive as a world community and not as fragmentized, isolated groups. After the experiences in our own time, it is naïve to believe that the treatment of Jews in one country has no influence upon the status of Jews in another, however far away. American anti-Semitism in the thirties was encouraged by Hitler's success, and Russian anti-Semitism at the turn of the century justified its aggressive policies with references to the anti-Semitic movements in Berlin and Paris.

As Jewish peoplehood has now become an accepted and important factor in the new battle for Jewish survival, so does Israel play a particularly significant part in our American Jewish existence. Its role is of such overriding importance that it must be clearly defined.

It is probably one of our unavoidable dilemmas that the symbol of our relationship with Israel is the check which represents our annual contribution. Israel accepts it because she could not exist without it. We give it because it seems to be an expression of our participation. Whether we wish so or not, it creates a relationship of benefactor and beneficiary, not the happiest of human relations. And not one to win friends. But we are not here concerned with a popularity contest. What is lacking on the part of many leaders of Is-

rael is the simple comprehension of the facts of Jewish
life in America, of the very special nature and structure of American Jewry. Some have suggested that
this lack of comprehension is due to the fact that
Israeli leaders rarely meet "American Jewry." They
are apt to meet leadership groups, fund raisers and
executive directors. It may not be easy to get a good
look at American Jewry when matters of contribution
and investments are discussed. Whatever the cause,
many of the statements on American Jewry which
emanate from Jerusalem reveal utter ignorance of the
American Jewish community.

The relationship between American Jewry and the
State of Israel suffers even more grievously from political considerations. The Zionist movement, as conceived by Herzl and developed by his successors, rec-
ognizes as its highest authority the Zionist Congress
convened by the World Zionist Organization. The congress, once the great international assembly of world
Jewry, is today, after the creation of the state, a strange
and curious conglomerate. Here are assembled the
Zionists from many countries of the world, together
with the official delegates of the political parties coming from the sovereign State of Israel. The party
delegates from Israel are in the majority. There is no
doubt that they and the political leaders of Israel determine the affairs of the Zionist movement. To be
sure, there are clashes of opinion, but most of them

result from the totally unclarified political situation, which has become so untenable. The whole construction makes little sense and is fraught with many dangers. Even the former Secretary of Foreign Affairs, Moshe Sharett, maintains that the preservation of the Israeli parties in the Diaspora no longer has any validity. But this is an understatement. It is politically impossible to maintain branches of political parties of a sovereign state outside of that state. Nobody interested in a clearly understood political status of the Jews in the countries of the world can want to perpetuate such a situation. For the sake of a new strong, well-founded relationship between American Jewry and Israel, this is intolerable. The Jews of the world, of which the Jews of Israel (not the political parties) are a part, should be represented in the World Jewish Congress, which holds international meetings every two years and deals most capably with every facet of Jewish problems. It ought not to, nor can it, determine the political decisions of the State of Israel. This must be done by Israel. It may criticize or agree with Israel. It must be an independent organ of world Jewry. We need, indeed, a Jewish Declaration of Political Independence from the State of Israel. This must be done for the sake of Israel and for the sake of world Jewry. The Zionist movement, responsible to a party-controlled Zionist Congress, cannot claim such independence.

This does not mean that American Jews should not take an active interest in the affairs of Israel, political and otherwise. But they can do this effectively only if they themselves have no political ties with any country other than their own. The participation of Jews from any other country in the election campaigns of Israel is preposterous. The very idea proposes some sort of schizophrenia, which is unhealthy for all concerned. Such abstention from Israeli politics should not stem from any fear of dual allegiance, which is the pet argument of insecure Jews who tremble at the very thought that Jewish interest in Israel may result in dire retributions. This fear is not shared by any other normal group in America. The Irish march down on Fifth Avenue, with Irish flags unfurled, and patriotic Irish songs shatter the American air on St. Patrick's Day without contaminating it. The Italians who are patriotic Americans intone the Italian anthem on Columbus Day, and in 1961 they proudly celebrated the hundredth anniversary of the unification of Italy. In the light of these manifestations of American generosity, it is foolish to accuse American Jews who are interested in Israel of high treason.

The Jews outside of Israel have a natural, moral and Jewish obligation to stand by Israel and help to meet all her needs, economic and political. At times, the political interests of Israel and those of our own country may clash. It is a farfetched possibility, but it might someday happen. In such an hour of painful dilemma and conflict, the Jews will side with the country in which they live. Nobody has any doubts about it, neither the Jews here nor the Israelis. It simply cannot be otherwise.

American Jewry must lose no time in building a relationship with Israel which will bear fruit in the next generation. This relationship cannot be merely political or material. The great test for the soundness of it will come when Israel is financially and politically independent. As soon as the need for fund raising ceases, American Jewry will be at a loss to find some new, meaningful relationship with Israel. Many thoughtful people in Israel hope for such a day of their own independence from world Jewry. Someday, they hope, they will pay their own bills, and then they will see whether American Jews will be interested in them. In the meantime American Jews, whose generosity has set an example to all Americans, postpone the day of reckoning with the thought that the Messiah has not yet come and that he is not likely to come "soon and in our day." Their attitude is "let the next generation think of new and different relationships with Israel."

But then it will be too late. The state will have developed. The people there, having had no real contacts with world Jewry, will be estranged. The new American Jewish generation, having heard of Israel only at fund-raising meetings or in political debates, will have no personal interest in the matter. Even today, less than fifteen years after the founding of the state, polls taken among Jewish students at the universities show a lack of enthusiasm for Israel. Sometimes there is a complete aloofness toward that "foreign state in the Near East." No emotional bonds exist. No personal contact has taken place. Of course, there are some groups, Zionist and non-Zionist, that have embarked upon some summer program. In some individual cases the program calls even for a longer period of stay in Israel. But what is urgently needed is a community plan in which all of Jewry participates. It will call for the mobilization of a great deal of money. But, above all, it will call for imagination and a rekindling of fervor and enthusiasm which might replace the dreamlike quality which has brought the state into being. Now that Israel exists, urgent needs are being discussed and met. But problems regarding drainage and road building can do little to fire the imagination of young people and create love for a faraway country.

American Jewish youth must come face to face with Israel and its people. In meeting the people, often so different from those in America, they will discover themselves, and the love which they will have for them will embrace all of Jewish life. Nobody who has ever seen Israel will deny that from here can come a regeneration of our own Jewish life. I have tried to show that self-affirmation of the Jew is the prerequisite for our continued existence. Israel as it is today, without falsification, with all its faults and greatness, can supply those wellsprings of a new Jewish experience. I doubt that anything else can.

We are too far removed from the unique features of Jewish life. We imitate Israeli dances and re-create its songs. But there on the land, in the settlements and even in the cities, in the country which has given birth to all that is great in Jewish heritage, it is genuine and immediate. Christians go to Jerusalem to retrace the steps of Christ on the Via Dolorosa. Why can't Jews have such pilgrimages, retracing in the living reality of the country the history of our people, and witnessing its resurrection firsthand? I shall never forget when, in 1934, the second year of the Hitler regime, I went to Palestine and found there a group of young Jewish children whose departure from Germany I had helped arrange. Rescued from death, they were laughing happily in their new home, a *kibbutz* situated near Mount Gilboa, where King Saul and Jonathan were killed in battle. While they were yet in Germany, I had told them this Biblical story. I now looked at the mountain with them, and I told them the story again, and suddenly, it leaped to life. Gilboa, Saul and Jonathan had become part of their daily existence. I am not suggesting that we can and must transplant American

Jewish youth to Israel, although I do not understand the shivering timidity with which some people (and even Zionists) talk about American Jewish pioneering. I am speaking here about the attempt to establish a personal, physical contact with Israel for those who will then return to America as more fervent Jews, regenerated and enriched for themselves, for the Jewish community and for their American life as well.

The most concrete and ambitious plan has come, not from American Jewry, but from David Ben-Gurion, who said in a remarkable speech delivered in December, 1961, in Jerusalem:

> It is the duty of those who, because of their age or economic situation, cannot come to Israel to send their young sons and daughters to study in Israel in a secondary school or university, even with personal obligation, to remain here for the rest of their lives. If American Jewry succeeded in sending here tens of thousands of young people to study for at least a year in Israeli schools without thereby wasting their time and losing their opportunities to study — it is clear that thousands of these young people, after seeing for themselves what the Jewish State has done and what it still has to do, would willingly and enthusiastically join the builders and workers.

Of course, the figures seem unrealistic, but that American youth, at a time when we speak of the Peace Corps, could be inspired to this type of personal service to Israel is beyond doubt. Naturally, it takes more than a speech to translate this Jewish pilgrimage plan into reality. If American Jewry would concentrate on this plan, we would have an answer not merely to the problem of Israeli-Jewish relationship but to the question of meaningful Jewish survival in the world as well.

It is amazing how many Jews who claim to be peripheral Jews feel the need somehow to "come home." Take, for example, the amazing spectacle of the modern Jewish artists. Few would call themselves Jewish survivalists. "The Jewish question," writes Karl Shapiro in the Introduction to his *Poems of a Jew*, "whatever it may be, is not my concern. Nor is Judaism. Nor is Jewry. Nor is Israel. The religious question is not my concern. . . . These poems, in any case, are not religious poems but poems of a Jew. No one has been able to define a Jew, and in essence this defiance of definition is the central meaning of Jewish consciousness." And then he proceeds to write the most exciting Jewish poems. And so it goes with painters and actors, with sculptors, writers and architects. Max Weber, the great American painter, discovers his Jewishness under the impact of Hitler, and Jewish Hassidim dance through his American paintings. Jacob Epstein chisels into the faces of his great statues the tragic experience of the Jew. The Italian genius Modigliani races through life without ever painting a Jewish subject, but with so much Jewish passion that he writes the name of one of his models in Hebrew letters across the canvas. Of course, Marc Chagall is full of his Jewish Vitebsk, but even in Pascin and in Chaim Soutine, in the sculptor Jacques Lipschitz, in American writers such as Philip Roth and Bernard Malamud, and in so many Jewish contemporary writers in Canada and England there is Jewish pathos and rejection and pain. This is a strange procession of Jewish return. They cannot escape Judaism because they cannot escape themselves. An artist must face himself or else he cannot write or paint or sculpt or sing. Again, self-discovery is the prime motivation. And this is not merely true of creative artists. It is true of the ordinary people as well. It shines through even the negativists and self-haters; they cannot escape, either.

But I admit that present conditions seem to speak against Jewish survival: the watering down of the Jewish heritage, the provincial mentality of the Jewish organized religion, the laziness, the rebellion of many against any interference with comfort and convenience, the lack of the kind of heroism and stubbornness that are required for conscious survival. In spite of all this, I believe that there will be a new kind of Jewish survival. Not one born of nightmares and fears. Not one born of dreams and illusions. But one born of a new twentieth-century understanding of man as he is, of all the factors, complexities, memories, drives and hopes that make of a human being something living, something so unbelievably rich and unique, so unlimited in desire and potential. For those to whom the collective memory of being a Jew is part of their personal possession, Jewish survival will become a matter of personal concern. They will want to understand and know themselves through the experience of Jewish history and even the Hebrew language. Without knowledge, the new Jewish generation will understand, there can be no Jewish survival. Those to whom Judaism is a way of believing and praying will find a faith which requires no compromise of intellectual honesty. Organized Jewish religion, if its leaders have any sense and understanding of the needs of the people, will begin to liberate itself from those kindergarten approaches which call for chocolate-flavored and sugar-coated Judaism, for easy-to-digest sermons and social hustle and bustle, and will yet come into its own. Judaism must divest itself of the sense of inferiority which has bedeviled and belittled it. As a minority religion, it must act and think and preach with the dignity and wisdom of the mother religion that it is. The Jews must celebrate their Hanukkah, not in the shadow of the Christmas tree, but with the knowledge that without the Maccabees there would have been neither Jesus nor Paul nor Christianity. They must not stare at the Easter celebration with envy, but sit around their Seder tables and sing of freedom, knowing that without the Exodus from Egypt which they celebrate, there would be no Ten Commandments, no Sabbath and no Sermon on the Mount. Judaism must and can — after so many centuries of blood and tears — become a proud and mature way of life.